C

POWER THROUGH PRAYER

E.M. BOUNDS

Devotional commentary
by Steve Uppal

ALL NATIONS
PUBLISHING

POWER THROUGH PRAYER
AN Publishing Classic Series

Power Through Prayer by Edward M. Bounds is public domain.

ISBN 978-1-7390986-8-1

Cover design by Naomi Moyo.

Printed by Short Run Press, Exeter, Devon, UK.

Dedicated to
the prayer warriors
of All Nations Wolverhampton
for standing in the gap

CONTENTS

Foreword

In an age of instant gratification and constant distractions, E.M. Bounds' *Power Through Prayer* stands as a powerful and timeless reminder of the essential role prayer plays in the life of every believer. Though written over a century ago, its message rings with fresh urgency today: without deep, consistent communion with God, our efforts – even in ministry – are powerless.

When I first encountered this book more than 20 years ago, I was struck by Bounds' passionate plea for believers, particularly those in leadership, to make prayer the bedrock of their spiritual life. His words challenged me to examine my own reliance on God, not just in moments of need, but as a daily practice. I was inspired by the stories of spiritual giants in history who shaped the cause of history through their prayer lives.

Bounds writes with a clarity and conviction that invites the reader into deeper, more sincere prayer. His insights are not theoretical, but practical and rooted in a deep love for God and a desire to see others transformed through prayer. Each chapter is both a challenge and a comfort, reminding us that God's power is made manifest through those who are willing to spend time in His presence.

As you read *Power Through Prayer*, my hope is that it will stir you as it has stirred countless others, calling you to a life of prayer that transforms not only your own heart but the world around you. May this book be a guide and a companion as you seek to know God more intimately through prayer.

Steve Uppal
September 2024

The Life of Edward M. Bounds

Edward McKendree Bounds was born on August 15th, 1835, in Missouri. After his father died while he was still a young teenager, he moved in with relatives in California to follow the gold rush. He returned to Missouri four years later to study law, having had no success at the mines. At 19, Bounds became the youngest practising lawyer in Missouri.

It was five years later, during the Third Great Awakening, that Bounds felt the call of God to devote himself fully to Christian Ministry. He promptly enrolled in the Centenary Seminary in Palmyra. Two years later, he was ordained and appointed pastor of the Monticello, Missouri Methodist Church.

During the American Civil War, the Union Army arrested pastors as though they were sympathisers with the Confederate Army. Although he was opposed to slavery, Bounds refused to sign the Oath of Allegiance as he viewed this as an act of the Federal state usurping Jesus Christ as the head of the church. He was also unable to pay the $500 bond required by the Union Army. He was therefore arrested and held prisoner in Franklin for 18 months.

Bounds was released in a prisoner exchange between the Union and the Confederacy. Moved by the spirit and valour of the soldiers he witnessed at the frontlines, he joined the Confederacy in 1863, at the age of 28. He was soon appointed officially as chaplain to the Confederate States Army. Despite having permission to take up duty in the rear and being provided a horse to ride to safety, Bounds distinguished himself to his men by accompanying them on the battlefield. He was constantly seen leading them on with shouts of encouragement, even while he was drawing enemy fire.

The Battle of Franklin was a particularly significant event for Bounds. The soldiers knew that the battle was the final stand for the South, and he anticipated that thousands would face certain death and the imminent prospect of encountering God. Longing for their salvation, he was desperately praying for them and fervently sharing the gospel, drawing alongside and helping wounded soldiers any way he could. Whilst many continued to mock, a good number were saved, and many people today still refer to this time as the Franklin revival.

At the Battle of Franklin, Bounds was badly wounded and taken prisoner. After his recovery, he was given the task of digging mass graves for the very soldiers he had lived with, led and ministered to. Many reported that as he dug, he would quote scripture, sing, and encourage his fellow captives.

Having signed an oath of loyalty to the government, he was released and allowed to return to his home state of Missouri. He obeyed and dutifully returned but his heart was still with the people of Franklin. There was a spiritual heaviness over Franklin that he could not ignore. He and many others recognised the importance of prayer in changing the spiritual atmosphere and help bring about recovery from the severe destruction and impact of the Civil War. In early 1865 after the end of the war, Bounds returned to help rebuild the towns of Franklin. He was troubled that soldiers lay in mass graves without the dignity of a proper burial and committed himself to the task of digging up the bodies and conducting individual burials, publishing the names of the deceased in the Missouri newspaper.

Recognising the spiritual darkness over the city, Bounds also stepped forward to fill the vacancy as pastor of the Franklin Methodist Episcopal Church South. He instigated weekly Tuesday evening prayer meetings with men from the community, which would extend for hours at a time, and which would bring about radical impact on the wider community of Franklin. This began to shape Bounds' understanding of the importance of prayer and its effect on daily life. As the community continued to pray for revival, a spiritual awakening began in the city. Hearts were touched, and the Spirit of God was poured out on many people. Bounds' church grew to over 500 in a matter of months and he was celebrated for leading the spiritual revival in Franklin.

Bounds travelled across America preaching and serving in many churches. He was most well-known for his heart for prayer and his thoughts on the importance of prayer in daily life. He was known for his personal commitment to pray every morning from 4am till 7am – and this was despite the complaints of his family members who shared the room! He wrote many books on the subject, most of which were published after he died and have since had a profound impact on the lives of many people worldwide, stirring countless people to take up the discipline of faithful, fervent prayer.

Throughout his ministry as an itinerant evangelist, he studied the Bible and wrote prodigiously. He was associate editor of the official Methodist newspaper for four years and was also editor of the St. Louis Christian Advocate for eight years. These roles helped spread the gospel across the nation and promoted his writing ministry, increasing the influence of his literature.

Bounds died at the age of 78 and was buried at Resthaven Cemetery. Both in his lifetime and till now, many have been inspired by his life and witness. His books and articles continue to have impact to this day. Bounds' radical obedience to God, his heart of compassion for people, the way he lived like Jesus, and his profound understanding of the importance of prayer are exemplary and leave us a challenging example to follow.

How to Use This Book

- Begin each chapter with prayer, asking the Holy Spirit to help you to understand and apply what you are about to learn.

- Use the notebook page to note down your reflections.

- Take your time and feel free to pause at any time and pray; there is no rush to complete the book. Take a moment to pause and pray if something stands out to you.

- Finish with prayer; ask the Holy Spirit to help you put into practice the things that you've learn. We want to be doers and not simply hearers (James 1:22).

- Take time to memorise one of the bible verses for each chapter and repeat it during the day and/or the coming week – it is both a resource for the future and a way of meditating prayerfully on the scripture.

1 Men[a] of Prayer Needed

We are constantly on a stretch, if not on a strain, to devise new methods, new plans, new organizations to advance the Church and secure enlargement and efficiency for the gospel. This trend of the day has a tendency to lose sight of the man or sink the man in the plan or organization. God's plan is to make much of the man, far more of him than of anything else. Men are God's method. The Church is looking for better methods; God is looking for better men.

"There was a man sent from God whose name was John." The dispensation that heralded and prepared the way for Christ was bound up in that man John. "Unto us a child is born, unto us a son is given." The world's salvation comes out of that cradled Son. When Paul appeals to the personal character of the men who rooted the gospel in the world, he solves the mystery of their success. The glory and efficiency of the gospel is staked on the men who proclaim it. When God declares that "the eyes of the Lord run to and fro throughout the whole earth, to show himself strong on the behalf of them whose heart is perfect toward him,"

---

[a] No changes to E.M. Bounds' book have been made apart from changes from US to UK spelling. We believe that the use of 'men' throughout the book refers to mankind, and that all men and women, married or single, can serve equally as leaders and in all ministries.

he declares the necessity of men and his dependence on them as a channel through which to exert his power upon the world. This vital, urgent truth is one that this age of machinery is apt to forget. The forgetting of it is as baneful on the work of God as would be the striking of the sun from his sphere. Darkness, confusion, and death would ensue.

What the Church needs to-day is not more machinery or better, not new organizations or more and novel methods, but men whom the Holy Ghost can use – men of prayer, men mighty in prayer. The Holy Ghost does not flow through methods, but through men. He does not come on machinery, but on men. He does not anoint plans, but men – men of prayer.

An eminent historian has said that the accidents of personal character have more to do with the revolutions of nations than either philosophic historians or democratic politicians will allow. This truth has its application in full to the gospel of Christ, the character and conduct of the followers of Christ – Christianize the world, transfigure nations and individuals. Of the preachers of the gospel it is eminently true.

The character as well as the fortunes of the gospel is committed to the preacher. He makes or mars the message from God to man. The preacher is the golden pipe through which the divine oil flows. The pipe must not only be golden, but open and flawless, that the oil may have a full, unhindered, unwasted flow.

The man makes the preacher. God must make the man. The messenger is, if possible, more than the message. The preacher is more than the sermon. The preacher makes the sermon. As the life-giving milk from the mother's bosom is but the mother's life, so all the preacher says is tinctured, impregnated by what the preacher is. The treasure is in earthen vessels, and the taste of the vessel impregnates and may discolour. The man, the whole man, lies behind the sermon. Preaching is not the performance of an hour. It is the outflow of a life. It takes twenty years to make a sermon, because it takes twenty years to make the man. The true sermon is a thing of life. The sermon grows because the man grows. The sermon is forceful because the man is forceful. The sermon is holy because the man is holy. The sermon is full of the divine unction because the man is full of the divine unction.

Paul termed it "My gospel;" not that he had degraded it by his personal eccentricities or diverted it by selfish appropriation, but the gospel was put into the heart and lifeblood of the man Paul, as a personal trust to be executed by his Pauline traits, to be set aflame and empowered by the fiery energy of his fiery soul. Paul's sermons – what were they? Where are they? Skeletons, scattered fragments, afloat on the sea of inspiration! But the man Paul, greater than his sermons, lives forever, in full form, feature and stature, with his moulding hand on the Church. The preaching is but a voice. The voice in silence dies, the text is forgotten, the sermon fades from memory; the preacher lives.

The sermon cannot rise in its life-giving forces above the man. Dead men give out dead sermons, and dead sermons kill. Everything depends on the spiritual character of the preacher. Under the Jewish dispensation the high priest had inscribed in jewelled letters on a golden frontlet: "Holiness to the Lord." So every preacher in Christ's ministry must be moulded into and mastered by this same holy motto. It is a crying shame for the Christian ministry to fall lower in holiness of character and holiness of aim than the Jewish priesthood. Jonathan Edwards said: "I went on with my eager pursuit after more holiness and conformity to Christ. The heaven I desired was a heaven of holiness."

The gospel of Christ does not move by popular waves. It has no self-propagating power. It moves as the men who have charge of it move. The preacher must impersonate the gospel. Its divine, most distinctive features must be embodied in him. The constraining power of love must be in the preacher as a projecting, eccentric, an all-commanding, self-oblivious force. The energy of self-denial must be his being, his heart and blood and bones. He must go forth as a man among men, clothed with humility, abiding in meekness, wise as a serpent, harmless as a dove; the bonds of a servant with the spirit of a king, a king in high, royal, in dependent bearing, with the simplicity and sweetness of a child. The preacher must throw himself, with all the abandon of a perfect, self-emptying faith and a self-consuming zeal, into his work for the salvation of men. Hearty, heroic, compassionate, fearless martyrs must the men be who take hold of and shape a generation for God. If they be timid time servers, place seekers, if they be men pleasers or men fearers, if their faith has a weak hold on God or his Word, if their denial be broken by any phase of self or the world, they cannot take hold of the Church nor the world for God.

The preacher's sharpest and strongest preaching should be to himself. His most difficult, delicate, laborious, and thorough work must be with himself. The training of the twelve was the great, difficult, and enduring work of Christ. Preachers are not sermon makers, but men makers and saint makers, and he only is well-trained for this business who has made himself a man and a saint. It is not great talents nor great learning nor great preachers that God needs, but men great in holiness, great in faith, great in love, great in fidelity, great for God – men always preaching by holy sermons in the pulpit, by holy lives out of it. These can mould a generation for God.

After this order, the early Christians were formed. Men they were of solid mould, preachers after the heavenly type – heroic, stalwart, soldierly, saintly. Preaching with them meant self-denying, self-crucifying, serious, toilsome, martyr business. They applied themselves to it in a way that told on their generation, and formed in its womb a generation yet unborn for God. The preaching man is to be the praying man. Prayer is the preacher's mightiest weapon. An almighty force in itself, it gives life and force to all.

The real sermon is made in the closet. The man – God's man – is made in the closet. His life and his profoundest convictions were born in his secret communion with God. The burdened and tearful agony of his spirit, his weightiest and sweetest messages were got when alone with God. Prayer makes the man; prayer makes the preacher; prayer makes the pastor.

The pulpit of this day is weak in praying. The pride of learning is against the dependent humility of prayer. Prayer is with the pulpit too often only official – a performance for the routine of service. Prayer is not to the modern pulpit the mighty force it was in Paul's life or Paul's ministry. Every preacher who does not make prayer a mighty factor in his own life and ministry is weak as a factor in God's work and is powerless to project God's cause in this world.

Reflect

How can you commit to becoming a person of prayer by dedicating specific times daily to pray earnestly? Perhaps consider having it as part of your morning routine, at the same time and the same place?

Pray

Father God, thank You for designing me for close communion with You. I choose to consecrate myself to pray daily. Search me, help me, mould me so that I may be a person of integrity, having a life that is consistent with the message You give me to speak. In Jesus' name I ask, amen.

Meditate

The effective, fervent prayer of a righteous man
avails much.
James 5:16 NKJV

My dear children, for whom I am again in the
pains of childbirth until Christ is formed in you,
Galatians 4:19 NIV

"I am the vine; you are the branches.
If you remain in me and I in you,
you will bear much fruit;
apart from me you can do nothing."
John 15:5 NIV

Notes

2 Our Sufficiency is of God

The sweetest graces by a slight perversion may bear the bitterest fruit. The sun gives life, but sunstrokes are death. Preaching is to give life; it may kill. The preacher holds the keys; he may lock as well as unlock. Preaching is God's great institution for the planting and maturing of spiritual life. When properly executed, its benefits are untold; when wrongly executed, no evil can exceed its damaging results. It is an easy matter to destroy the flock if the shepherd be unwary or the pasture be destroyed, easy to capture the citadel if the watchmen be asleep or the food and water be poisoned. Invested with such gracious prerogatives, exposed to so great evils, involving so many grave responsibilities, it would be a parody on the shrewdness of the devil and a libel on his character and reputation if he did not bring his master influences to adulterate the preacher and the preaching. In face of all this, the exclamatory interrogatory of Paul, "Who is sufficient for these things?" is never out of order.

Paul says: "Our sufficiency is of God, who also hath made us able ministers of the New Testament; not of the letter, but of the spirit: for the letter kills, but the spirit gives life." The true ministry is God-touched, God-enabled, and God-made. The Spirit of God is on the preacher in anointing power, the fruit of the Spirit is in his heart, the Spirit of God has vitalized the man and the word; his preaching gives life, gives life as the spring gives life; gives life as the resurrection gives life;

gives ardent life as the summer gives ardent life; gives fruitful life as the autumn gives fruitful life. The life-giving preacher is a man of God, whose heart is ever athirst for God, whose soul is ever following hard after God, whose eye is single to God, and in whom by the power of God's Spirit the flesh and the world have been crucified and his ministry is like the generous flood of a life-giving river.

The preaching that kills is non-spiritual preaching. The ability of the preaching is not from God. Lower sources than God have given to it energy and stimulant. The Spirit is not evident in the preacher nor his preaching. Many kinds of forces may be projected and stimulated by preaching that kills, but they are not spiritual forces. They may resemble spiritual forces, but are only the shadow, the counterfeit; life they may seem to have, but the life is magnetized. The preaching that kills is the letter; shapely and orderly it may be, but it is the letter still, the dry, husky letter, the empty, bald shell. The letter may have the germ of life in it, but it has no breath of spring to evoke it; winter seeds they are, as hard as the winter's soil, as icy as the winter's air, no thawing nor germinating by them. This letter-preaching has the truth. But even divine truth has no life-giving energy alone; it must be energized by the Spirit, with all God's forces at its back. Truth unquickened by God's Spirit deadens as much as, or more than, error. It may be the truth without admixture; but without the Spirit its shade and touch are deadly, its truth error, its light darkness.

The letter-preaching is unctionless, neither mellowed nor oiled by the Spirit. There may be tears, but tears cannot run God's machinery; tears may be but summer's breath on a snow-covered iceberg, nothing but surface slush. Feelings and earnestness there may be, but it is the emotion of the actor and the earnestness of the attorney. The preacher may feel from the kindling of his own sparks, be eloquent over his own exegesis, earnest in delivering the product of his own brain; the professor may usurp the place and imitate the fire of the apostle; brains and nerves may serve the place and feign the work of God's Spirit, and by these forces the letter may glow and sparkle like an illumined text, but the glow and sparkle will be as barren of life as the field sown with pearls. The death-dealing element lies back of the words, back of the sermon, back of the occasion, back of the manner, back of the action.

The great hindrance is in the preacher himself. He has not in himself the mighty life-creating forces. There may be no discount on his orthodoxy, honesty, cleanness, or earnestness; but somehow the man, the inner man, in its secret places has never broken down and surrendered to God, his inner life is not a great highway for the transmission of God's message, God's power. Somehow self and not God rules in the holy of holiest. Somewhere, all unconscious to himself, some spiritual non-conductor has touched his inner being, and the divine current has been arrested. His inner being has never felt its thorough spiritual bankruptcy, its utter powerlessness; he has never learned to cry out with an ineffable cry of self-despair and self-helplessness till God's power and God's fire comes in and fills, purifies, empowers. Self-esteem, self-ability in some pernicious shape has defamed and violated the temple which should be held sacred for God. Life-giving preaching costs the preacher much – death to self, crucifixion to the world, the travail of his own soul. Crucified preaching only can give life. Crucified preaching can come only from a crucified man.

Reflect

How can you prioritise developing your inner spiritual life over outward activities? Memorising the first beatitude could help as being 'poor in spirit' (Matthew 5:3) means being absolutely dependent on God.

Pray

Father God, thank You that Your Spirit gives me life and breathes life into all I do and say. Help me to rely on You and surrender myself to You in the secret place, so that my words and actions may have more significance in the public place. In Jesus' name I ask, amen.

Meditate

Not that we are sufficient of ourselves to think of anything as being from ourselves,
but our sufficiency is from God.
2 Corinthians 3:5 NKJV

Then He said to them all: "Whoever wants to be my disciple must deny themselves and
take up their cross daily and follow me.
Luke 9:23 NIV

For the kingdom of God is not a matter of talk but of power.
1 Corinthians 4:20 NIV

Notes

3 The Letter Kills

The preaching that kills may be, and often is, orthodox – dogmatically, inviolably orthodox. We love orthodoxy. It is good. It is the best. It is the clean, clear-cut teaching of God's Word, the trophies won by truth in its conflict with error, the levees which faith has raised against the desolating floods of honest or reckless misbelief or unbelief; but orthodoxy, clear and hard as crystal, suspicious and militant, may be but the letter well-shaped, well-named, and well-learned, the letter which kills. Nothing is so dead as a dead orthodoxy, too dead to speculate, too dead to think, to study, or to pray.

The preaching that kills may have insight and grasp of principles, may be scholarly and critical in taste, may have every minutia of the derivation and grammar of the letter, may be able to trim the letter into its perfect pattern, and illume it as Plato and Cicero may be illumined, may study it as a lawyer studies his text-books to form his brief or to defend his case, and yet be like a frost, a killing frost. Letter-preaching may be eloquent, enamelled with poetry and rhetoric, sprinkled with prayer spiced with sensation, illumined by genius and yet these be but the massive or chaste, costly mountings, the rare and beautiful flowers which coffin the corpse. The preaching which kills may be without scholarship, unmarked by any freshness of thought or feeling, clothed in tasteless generalities or vapid specialties, with style irregular, slovenly, savouring neither of closet nor of study, graced neither by thought, expression, or prayer. Under such preaching how wide and utter the desolation! how profound the spiritual death!

This letter-preaching deals with the surface and shadow of things, and not the things themselves. It does not penetrate the inner part. It has no deep insight into, no strong grasp of, the hidden life of God's Word. It is true to the outside, but the outside is the hull which must be broken and penetrated for the kernel. The letter may be dressed so as to attract and be fashionable, but the attraction is not toward God nor is the fashion for heaven. The failure is in the preacher. God has not made him. He has never been in the hands of God like clay in the hands of the potter. He has been busy about the sermon, its thought and finish, its drawing and impressive forces; but the deep things of God have never been sought, studied, fathomed, experienced by him. He has never stood before "the throne high and lifted up," never heard the seraphim song, never seen the vision nor felt the rush of that awful holiness, and cried out in utter abandon and despair under the sense of weakness and guilt, and had his life renewed, his heart touched, purged, inflamed by the live coal from God's altar. His ministry may draw people to him, to the Church, to the form and ceremony; but no true drawings to God, no sweet, holy, divine communion induced. The Church has been frescoed but not edified, pleased but not sanctified. Life is suppressed; a chill is on the summer air; the soil is baked. The city of our God becomes the city of the dead; the Church a graveyard, not an embattled army. Praise and prayer are stifled; worship is dead. The preacher and the preaching have helped sin, not holiness; peopled hell, not heaven.

Preaching which kills is prayerless preaching. Without prayer the preacher creates death, and not life. The preacher who is feeble in prayer is feeble in life-giving forces. The preacher who has retired prayer as a conspicuous and largely prevailing element in his own character has shorn his preaching of its distinctive life-giving power. Professional praying there is and will be, but professional praying helps the preaching to its deadly work. Professional praying chills and kills both preaching and praying. Much of the lax devotion and lazy, irreverent attitudes in congregational praying are attributable to professional praying in the pulpit. Long, discursive, dry, and inane are the prayers in many pulpits. Without unction or heart, they fall like a killing frost on all the graces of worship. Death-dealing prayers they are. Every vestige of devotion has perished under their breath. The deader they are the longer they grow. A plea for short praying, live praying, real heart praying, praying by the Holy Spirit – direct, specific, ardent, simple, unctuous in the pulpit –

is in order. A school to teach preachers how to pray, as God counts praying, would be more beneficial to true piety, true worship, and true preaching than all theological schools.

Stop! Pause! Consider! Where are we? What are we doing? Preaching to kill? Praying to kill? Praying to God! the great God, the Maker of all worlds, the Judge of all men! What reverence! what simplicity! what sincerity! what truth in the inward parts is demanded! How real we must be! How hearty! Prayer to God the noblest exercise, the loftiest effort of man, the most real thing! Shall we not discard forever accursed preaching that kills and prayer that kills, and do the real thing, the mightiest thing – prayerful praying, life-creating preaching, bring the mightiest force to bear on heaven and earth and draw on God's exhaustless and open treasure for the need and beggary of man?

Reflect

How can you focus on the spirit of prayer rather than just the form, ensuring your prayers are heartfelt and genuine? Remember that the Holy Spirit is your helper, and he is right there with you (John 14:26). Are there any unhelpful formalities in your prayer life that need reconsidering?

Pray

Father God, forgive me for not valuing the power and importance of prayer. Forgive me for living a powerless Christian life. Give me the grace to pray and pursue you wholeheartedly. In Jesus' name I ask, amen.

Meditate

"God is Spirit, and those who worship Him
must worship in spirit and truth."
John 4:24 NKJV

In the same way, the Spirit helps us
in our weakness. We do not know what we ought
to pray for, but the Spirit himself intercedes for us
through wordless groans.
Romans 8:26 NIV

Notes

4 Tendencies to Be Avoided

There are two extreme tendencies in the ministry. The one is to shut itself out from intercourse with the people. The monk, the hermit were illustrations of this; they shut themselves out from men to be more with God. They failed, of course. Our being with God is of use only as we expend its priceless benefits on men. This age, neither with preacher nor with people, is much intent on God. Our hankering is not that way. We shut ourselves to our study, we become students, bookworms, Bible worms, sermon makers, noted for literature, thought, and sermons; but the people and God, where are they? Out of heart, out of mind. Preachers who are great thinkers, great students must be the greatest of prayers, or else they will be the greatest of backsliders, heartless professionals, rationalistic, less than the least of preachers in God's estimate.

The other tendency is to thoroughly popularize the ministry. He is no longer God's man, but a man of affairs, of the people. He prays not, because his mission is to the people. If he can move the people, create an interest, a sensation in favour of religion, an interest in Church work – he is satisfied. His personal relation to God is no factor in his work. Prayer has little or no place in his plans. The disaster and ruin of such a ministry cannot be computed by earthly arithmetic.

What the preacher is in prayer to God, for himself, for his people, so is his power for real good to men, so is his true fruitfulness, his true fidelity to God, to man, for time, for eternity.

It is impossible for the preacher to keep his spirit in harmony with the divine nature of his high calling without much prayer. That the preacher by dint of duty and laborious fidelity to the work and routine of the ministry can keep himself in trim and fitness is a serious mistake. Even sermon-making, incessant and taxing as an art, as a duty, as a work, or as a pleasure, will engross and harden, will estrange the heart, by neglect of prayer, from God. The scientist loses God in nature. The preacher may lose God in his sermon.

Prayer freshens the heart of the preacher, keeps it in tune with God and in sympathy with the people, lifts his ministry out of the chilly air of a profession, fructifies routine and moves every wheel with the facility and power of a divine unction.

Mr. Spurgeon says: "Of course the preacher is above all others distinguished as a man of prayer. He prays as an ordinary Christian, else he were a hypocrite. He prays more than ordinary Christians, else he were disqualified for the office he has undertaken. If you as ministers are not very prayerful, you are to be pitied. If you become lax in sacred devotion, not only will you need to be pitied but your people also, and the day cometh in which you shall be ashamed and confounded. All our libraries and studies are mere emptiness compared with our closets. Our seasons of fasting and prayer at the Tabernacle have been high days indeed; never has heaven's gate stood wider; never have our hearts been nearer the central Glory."

The praying which makes a prayerful ministry is not a little praying put in as we put flavour to give it a pleasant smack, but the praying must be in the body, and form the blood and bones. Prayer is no petty duty, put into a corner; no piecemeal performance made out of the fragments of time which have been snatched from business and other engagements of life; but it means that the best of our time, the heart of our time and strength must be given. It does not mean the closet absorbed in the study or swallowed up in the activities of ministerial duties; but it means the closet first, the study and activities second, both study and activities freshened and made efficient by the closet. Prayer that affects one's ministry must give tone to one's life. The praying which gives colour and bent to character is no pleasant, hurried pastime. It must enter as strongly into the heart and life as Christ's "strong crying and tears" did; must draw out the soul into an agony of desire as Paul's did; must be an inwrought fire and force like the "effectual, fervent prayer" of James; must be of that quality which, when put into the golden censer and incensed before God, works mighty spiritual throes and revolutions.

Prayer is not a little habit pinned on to us while we were tied to our mother's apron strings; neither is it a little decent quarter of a minute's grace said over an hour's dinner, but it is a most serious work of our most serious years. It engages more of time and appetite than our longest dinings or richest feasts. The prayer that makes much of our preaching must be made much of. The character of our praying will determine the character of our preaching. Light praying will make light preaching. Prayer makes preaching strong, gives it unction, and makes it stick. In every ministry weighty for good, prayer has always been a serious business.

The preacher must be pre-eminently a man of prayer. His heart must graduate in the school of prayer. In the school of prayer only can the heart learn to preach. No learning can make up for the failure to pray. No earnestness, no diligence, no study, no gifts will supply its lack.

Talking to men for God is a great thing, but talking to God for men is greater still. He will never talk well and with real success to men for God who has not learned well how to talk to God for men. More than this, prayerless words in the pulpit and out of it are deadening words.

Reflect

What steps can you take to avoid distractions and superficiality in prayer, striving for deep, meaningful communication with God? Perhaps ensuring no digital devices are near you during your prayer time, or making sure all devices are on 'do not disturb' mode until your prayer time is complete?

Pray

Father God, search me and cleanse me from anything that keeps me from being wholly united with You in prayer. Help me to stay in tune and in step with Your Spirit so that it is Your life that flows out into all that I do and say. In Jesus' name I ask, amen.

Meditate

Be sober, be vigilant; because your adversary
the devil walks about like a roaring lion,
seeking whom he may devour.
1 Peter 5:8 NKJV

Therefore, my beloved, just as you have always
obeyed me, not only in my presence, but much
more now in my absence, work out your own
salvation with fear and trembling; for it is God
who is at work in you, enabling you both to will
and to work for his good pleasure.
Philippians 2:12-13 NRSV

Notes

5 Prayer, the Great Essential

Prayer, in the preacher's life, in the preacher's study, in the preacher's pulpit, must be a conspicuous and an all-impregnating force and an all-colouring ingredient. It must play no secondary part, be no mere coating. To him it is given to be with his Lord "all night in prayer." The preacher, to train himself in self-denying prayer, is charged to look to his Master, who, "rising up a great while before day, went out, and departed into a solitary place, and there prayed."

The preacher's study ought to be a closet, a Bethel, an altar, a vision, and a ladder, that every thought might ascend heavenward ere it went manward; that every part of the sermon might be scented by the air of heaven and made serious, because God was in the study.

As the engine never moves until the fire is kindled, so preaching, with all its machinery, perfection, and polish, is at a dead standstill, as far as spiritual results are concerned, till prayer has kindled and created the steam. The texture, fineness, and strength of the sermon is as so much rubbish unless the mighty impulse of prayer is in it, through it, and behind it. The preacher must, by prayer, put God in the sermon.

The preacher must, by prayer, move God toward the people before he can move the people to God by his words. The preacher must have had audience and ready access to God before he can have access to the people. An open way to God for the preacher is the surest pledge of an open way to the people.

It is necessary to iterate and reiterate that prayer, as a mere habit, as a performance gone through by routine or in a professional way, is a dead and rotten thing. Such praying has no connection with the praying for which we plead. We are stressing true praying, which engages and sets on fire every high element of the preacher's being – prayer which is born of vital oneness with Christ and the fullness of the Holy Ghost, which springs from the deep, overflowing fountains of tender compassion, deathless solicitude for man's eternal good; a consuming zeal for the glory of God; a thorough conviction of the preacher's difficult and delicate work and of the imperative need of God's mightiest help. Praying grounded on these solemn and profound convictions is the only true praying. Preaching backed by such praying is the only preaching which sows the seeds of eternal life in human hearts and builds men up for heaven.

It is true that there may be popular preaching, pleasant preaching, taking preaching, preaching of much intellectual, literary, and brainy force, with its measure and form of good, with little or no praying; but the preaching which secures God's end in preaching must be born of prayer from text to exordium, delivered with the energy and spirit of prayer, followed and made to germinate, and kept in vital force in the hearts of the hearers by the preacher's prayers, long after the occasion has past.

We may excuse the spiritual poverty of our preaching in many ways, but the true secret will be found in the lack of urgent prayer for God's presence in the power of the Holy Spirit. There are preachers innumerable who can deliver masterful sermons after their order; but the effects are short-lived and do not enter as a factor at all into the regions of the spirit where the fearful war between God and Satan, heaven and hell, is being waged because they are not made powerfully militant and spiritually victorious by prayer.

The preachers who gain mighty results for God are the men who have prevailed in their pleadings with God ere venturing to plead with men. The preachers who are the mightiest in their closets with God are the mightiest in their pulpits with men.

Preachers are human folks, and are exposed to and often caught by the strong driftings of human currents. Praying is spiritual work; and human nature does not like taxing, spiritual work. Human nature wants to sail to heaven under a favouring breeze, a full, smooth sea.

Prayer is humbling work. It abases intellect and pride, crucifies vainglory, and signs our spiritual bankruptcy, and all these are hard for flesh and blood to bear. It is easier not to pray than to bear them. So we come to one of the crying evils of these times, maybe of all times – little or no praying. Of these two evils, perhaps little praying is worse than no praying. Little praying is a kind of make-believe, a salvo for the conscience, a farce and a delusion.

The little estimate we put on prayer is evident from the little time we give to it. The time given to prayer by the average preacher scarcely counts in the sum of the daily aggregate. Not infrequently the preacher's only praying is by his bedside in his nightdress, ready for bed and soon in it, with, perchance the addition of a few hasty snatches of prayer ere he is dressed in the morning. How feeble, vain, and little is such praying compared with the time and energy devoted to praying by holy men in and out of the Bible! How poor and mean our petty, childish praying is beside the habits of the true men of God in all ages! To men who think praying their main business and devote time to it according to this high estimate of its importance does God commit the keys of his kingdom, and by them does he work his spiritual wonders in this world. Great praying is the sign and seal of God's great leaders and the earnest of the conquering forces with which God will crown their labours.

The preacher is commissioned to pray as well as to preach. His mission is incomplete if he does not do both well. The preacher may speak with all the eloquence of men and of angels; but unless he can pray with a faith which draws all heaven to his aid, his preaching will be "as sounding brass or a tinkling cymbal" for permanent God-honouring, soul-saving uses.

Reflect

How can you make prayer a non-negotiable part of your daily routine, recognising its essential role in your spiritual life? One way could be making a commitment to not leave the house until you have had time with the Lord. Would it help to have an accountability friend, someone you check in with to let them know how this commitment is going?

Pray

Father God, I recognize that prayer and personal transformation is my first and primary calling to You. Forgive me for the times I have not protected my prayer time with You from the busyness of doing life and ministry. Grow my appetite for staying in Your presence. In Jesus' name I ask, amen.

Meditate

Be anxious for nothing, but in everything
by prayer and supplication, with thanksgiving,
let your requests be made known to God.
Philippians 4:6 NKJV

...but because Jesus lives forever,
he has a permanent priesthood.
Therefore he is able to save completely those who
come to God through him, because he always
lives to intercede for them.
Hebrews 7:24-25 NIV

Notes

6 A Praying Ministry Successful

It may be put down as a spiritual axiom that in every truly successful ministry prayer is an evident and controlling force – evident and controlling in the life of the preacher, evident and controlling in the deep spirituality of his work. A ministry may be a very thoughtful ministry without prayer; the preacher may secure fame and popularity without prayer; the whole machinery of the preacher's life and work may be run without the oil of prayer or with scarcely enough to grease one cog; but no ministry can be a spiritual one, securing holiness in the preacher and in his people, without prayer being made an evident and controlling force.

The preacher that prays indeed puts God into the work. God does not come into the preacher's work as a matter of course or on general principles, but he comes by prayer and special urgency. That God will be found of us in the day that we seek him with the whole heart is as true of the preacher as of the penitent. A prayerful ministry is the only ministry that brings the preacher into sympathy with the people. Prayer as essentially unites to the human as it does to the divine. A prayerful ministry is the only ministry qualified for the high offices and responsibilities of the preacher. Colleges, learning, books, theology, preaching cannot make a preacher, but praying does. The apostles' commission to preach was a blank till filled up by the Pentecost which praying brought. A prayerful minister has passed beyond the regions of the popular, beyond the man of mere affairs, of secularities, of pulpit attractiveness; passed beyond the ecclesiastical organizer or general into a sublimer and mightier region, the region of the spiritual. Holiness is the product of his work; transfigured hearts and lives emblazon the reality of his work, its trueness and substantial nature. God is with him. His ministry is not projected on worldly or surface principles. He is deeply stored with and deeply schooled in the things of God. His long, deep communings with God about his people and the agony of his wrestling spirit have crowned him as a prince in the things of God. The iciness of the mere professional has long since melted under the intensity of his praying.

The superficial results of many a ministry, the deadness of others, are to be found in the lack of praying. No ministry can succeed without much praying, and this praying must be fundamental, ever-abiding, ever-increasing. The text, the sermon, should be the result of prayer. The study should be bathed in prayer, all its duties so impregnated with prayer, its whole spirit the spirit of prayer. "I am sorry that I have prayed so little," was the deathbed regret of one of God's chosen ones, a sad and remorseful regret for a preacher. "I want a life of greater, deeper, truer prayer," said the late Archbishop Tait. So may we all say, and this may we all secure.

God's true preachers have been distinguished by one great feature: they were men of prayer. Differing often in many things, they have always had a common centre. They may have started from different points, and travelled by different roads, but they converged to one point: they were one in prayer. God to them was the centre of attraction, and prayer was the path that led to God. These men prayed not occasionally, not a little at regular or at odd times; but they so prayed that their prayers entered into and shaped their characters; they so prayed as to affect their own lives and the lives of others; they so prayed as to make the history of the Church and influence the current of the times. They spent much time in prayer, not because they marked the shadow on the dial or the hands on the clock, but because it was to them so momentous and engaging a business that they could scarcely give over.

Prayer was to them what it was to Paul, a striving with earnest effort of soul; what it was to Jacob, a wrestling and prevailing; what it was to Christ, "strong crying and tears." They "prayed always with all prayer and supplication in the Spirit, and watching thereunto with all perseverance." "The effectual, fervent prayer" has been the mightiest weapon of God's mightiest soldiers. The statement in regard to Elijah – that he "was a man subject to like passions as we are, and he prayed earnestly that it might not rain: and it rained not on the earth by the space of three years and six months. And he prayed again, and the heaven gave rain, and the earth brought forth her fruit" – comprehends all prophets and preachers who have moved their generation for God, and shows the instrument by which they worked their wonders.

Reflect

Shall we develop a habit of spending significant time in prayer before any ministry work or preaching? This could be an hour before a service or concerted prayer effort in the few weeks leading up to an event or a major decision.

Pray

Holy Spirit, forgive me for the times when I have been quick to turn to manmade ideas and methods. Thank You for being my Helper. Teach me to pray the deep things of God and help me to wait on Him in prayer. May You only increase, and I decrease. In Jesus' name I ask, amen.

Meditate

Pray without ceasing, give thanks in all circumstances; for this is the will of God in Christ Jesus for you.

1 Thessalonians 5:17-18 ESV

"Now this is eternal life: that they know you, the only true God, and Jesus Christ, whom you have sent."

John 17:3 NIV

Notes

7 Much Time Should Be Given to Prayer

While many private prayers, in the nature of things, must be short; while public prayers, as a rule, ought to be short and condensed; while there is ample room for and value put on ejaculatory prayer – yet in our private communions with God time is a feature essential to its value. Much time spent with God is the secret of all successful praying.

Prayer which is felt as a mighty force is the mediate or immediate product of much time spent with God. Our short prayers owe their point and efficiency to the long ones that have preceded them. The short prevailing prayer cannot be prayed by one who has not prevailed with God in a mightier struggle of long continuance. Jacob's victory of faith could not have been gained without that all-night wrestling. God's acquaintance is not made by pop calls. God does not bestow his gifts on the casual or hasty comers and goers. Much with God alone is the secret of knowing him and of influence with him. He yields to the persistency of a faith that knows him. He bestows his richest gifts upon those who declare their desire for and appreciation of those gifts by the constancy as well as earnestness of their importunity. Christ, who in this as well as other things is our Example, spent many whole nights in prayer. His custom was to pray much. He had his habitual place to pray. Many long seasons of praying make up his history and character. Paul prayed day and night. It took time from very important interests for

Daniel to pray three times a day. David's morning, noon, and night praying were doubtless on many occasions very protracted. While we have no specific account of the time these Bible saints spent in prayer, yet the indications are that they consumed much time in prayer, and on some occasions long seasons of praying was their custom.

We would not have any think that the value of their prayers is to be measured by the clock, but our purpose is to impress on our minds the necessity of being much alone with God; and that if this feature has not been produced by our faith, then our faith is of a feeble and surface type.

The men who have most fully illustrated Christ in their character, and have most powerfully affected the world for him, have been men who spent so much time with God as to make it a notable feature of their lives. Charles Simeon devoted the hours from four till eight in the morning to God. Mr. Wesley spent two hours daily in prayer. He began at four in the morning. Of him, one who knew him well wrote: "He thought prayer to be more his business than anything else, and I have seen him come out of his closet with a serenity of face next to shining." John Fletcher stained the walls of his room by the breath of his prayers. Sometimes he would pray all night; always, frequently, and with great earnestness. His whole life was a life of prayer. "I would not rise from my seat," he said, "without lifting my heart to God." His greeting to a friend was always: "Do I meet you praying?" Luther said: "If I fail to spend two hours in prayer each morning, the devil gets the victory through the day. I have so much business I cannot get on without spending three hours daily in prayer." He had a motto: "He that has prayed well has studied well."

Archbishop Leighton was so much alone with God that he seemed to be in a perpetual meditation. "Prayer and praise were his business and his pleasure," says his biographer. Bishop Ken was so much with God that his soul was said to be God-enamoured. He was with God before the clock struck three every morning. Bishop Asbury said: "I propose to rise at four o'clock as often as I can and spend two hours in prayer and meditation." Samuel Rutherford, the fragrance of whose piety is still rich, rose at three in the morning to meet God in prayer. Joseph Alleine arose at four o'clock for his business of praying till eight. If he heard other tradesmen plying their business before he was up, he would exclaim: "O how this shames me! Doth not my Master deserve more than theirs?" He who has learned this trade well draws at will, on sight, and with acceptance of heaven's unfailing bank.

One of the holiest and among the most gifted of Scotch preachers says: "I ought to spend the best hours in communion with God. It is my noblest and most fruitful employment, and is not to be thrust into a corner. The morning hours, from six to eight, are the most uninterrupted and should be thus employed.

After tea is my best hour, and that should be solemnly dedicated to God. I ought not to give up the good old habit of prayer before going to bed; but guard must be kept against sleep. When I awake in the night, I ought to rise and pray. A little time after breakfast might be given to intercession." This was the praying plan of Robert McCheyne. The memorable Methodist band in their praying shame us. "From four to five in the morning, private prayer; from five to six in the evening, private prayer."

John Welch, the holy and wonderful Scotch preacher, thought the day ill spent if he did not spend eight or ten hours in prayer. He kept a plaid that he might wrap himself when he arose to pray at night. His wife would complain when she found him lying on the ground weeping. He would reply: "O woman, I have the souls of three thousand to answer for, and I know not how it is with many of them!"

Reflect

How can you allocate more time for prayer each day, understanding that quality time with God is crucial? As you may have established a morning routine by now, would it help in having an evening routine of journaling and prayer? Or perhaps setting aside time for a lunchtime prayer walk or using your commute time to pray?

Pray

Father God, I give the hours of my day to You. Please show me how I might spend more time in conversation with You. Give me the grace to obey You anytime You call, and to press through with You in intercessory prayer. In Jesus' name I ask, amen.

Meditate

Now in the morning, having risen a long while
before daylight, He went out and departed
to a solitary place; and there He prayed.
Mark 1:35 NKJV

This Book of the Law shall not depart from your
mouth, but you shall meditate on it day and night,
so that you may be careful to do
according to all that is written in it.
For then you will make your way prosperous,
and then you will have good success.
Joshua 1:8 ESV

Notes

8 Examples of Praying Men

Bishop Wilson says: "In H. Martyn's journal the spirit of prayer, the time he devoted to the duty, and his fervour in it are the first things which strike me."

Payson wore the hard-wood boards into grooves where his knees pressed so often and so long. His biographer says: "His continuing instant in prayer, be his circumstances what they might, is the most noticeable fact in his history, and points out the duty of all who would rival his eminency. To his ardent and persevering prayers must no doubt be ascribed in a great measure his distinguished and almost uninterrupted success."

The Marquis DeRenty, to whom Christ was most precious, ordered his servant to call him from his devotions at the end of half an hour. The servant at the time saw his face through an aperture. It was marked with such holiness that he hated to arouse him. His lips were moving, but he was perfectly silent. He waited until three half hours had passed; then he called to him, when he arose from his knees, saying that the half hour was so short when he was communing with Christ.

Brainerd said: "I love to be alone in my cottage, where I can spend much time in prayer."

William Bramwell is famous in Methodist annals for personal holiness and for his wonderful success in preaching and for the marvellous answers to his prayers. For hours at a time he would pray. He almost lived on his knees. He went over his circuits like a flame of fire. The fire was kindled by the time he spent in prayer. He often spent as much as four hours in a single season of prayer in retirement.

Bishop Andrewes spent the greatest part of five hours every day in prayer and devotion.

Sir Henry Havelock always spent the first two hours of each day alone with God. If the encampment was struck at 6 A.M., he would rise at four.

Earl Cairns rose daily at six o'clock to secure an hour and a half for the study of the Bible and for prayer, before conducting family worship at a quarter to eight.

Dr. Judson's success in prayer is attributable to the fact that he gave much time to prayer. He says on this point: "Arrange thy affairs, if possible, so that thou canst leisurely devote two or three hours every day not merely to devotional exercises but to the very act of secret prayer and communion with God. Endeavor seven times a day to withdraw from business and company and lift up thy soul to God in private retirement. Begin the day by rising after midnight and devoting some time amid the silence and darkness of the night to this sacred work. Let the hour of opening dawn find thee at the same work. Let the hours of nine, twelve, three, six, and nine at night witness the same. Be resolute in his cause. Make all practicable sacrifices to maintain it. Consider that thy time is short, and that business and company must not be allowed to rob thee of thy God." Impossible, say we, fanatical directions! Dr. Judson impressed an empire for Christ and laid the foundations of God's kingdom with imperishable granite in the heart of Burmah. He was successful, one of the few men who mightily impressed the world for Christ. Many men of greater gifts and genius and learning than he have made no such impression; their religious work is like footsteps in the sands, but he has engraved his work on the adamant. The secret of its profundity and endurance is found in the fact that he gave time to prayer. He kept the iron red-hot with prayer, and God's skill fashioned it with enduring power. No man can do a great and enduring work for God who is not a man of prayer, and no man can be a man of prayer who does not give much time to praying.

Is it true that prayer is simply the compliance with habit, dull and mechanical? A petty performance into which we are trained till tameness, shortness, superficiality are its chief elements? "Is it true that prayer is, as is assumed, little else than the half-passive play of sentiment which flows languidly on through the minutes or hours of easy reverie?"

Canon Liddon continues: "Let those who have really prayed give the answer. They sometimes describe prayer with the patriarch Jacob as a wrestling together with an Unseen Power which may last, not unfrequently in an earnest life, late into the night hours, or even to the break of day. Sometimes they refer to common intercession with St. Paul as a concerted struggle. They have, when praying, their eyes fixed on the Great Intercessor in Gethsemane, upon the drops of blood which fall to the ground in that agony of resignation and sacrifice. Importunity is of the essence of successful prayer. Importunity means not dreaminess but sustained work. It is through prayer especially that the kingdom of heaven suffereth violence and the violent take it by force. It was a saying of the late Bishop Hamilton that "No man is likely to do much good in prayer who does not begin by looking upon it in the light of a work to be prepared for and persevered in with all the earnestness which we bring to bear upon subjects which are in our opinion at once most interesting and most necessary."

Reflect

How can you emulate the dedication and fervour of great prayer warriors in history? Consider studying their lives by reading short articles or biographies of some of the examples given. Rather than being overwhelmed by their commitment, pick one thing that inspires you and see how you can adapt it to your life.

Pray

Father God, thank You for setting me in a family of great prayer warriors. As I follow their example, do a work in my heart so I can keep resolutely on this prayer journey I have begun with You. In Jesus' name I ask, amen.

Meditate

Thus the LORD used to speak to Moses face to
face, as one speaks to a friend. Then he would
return to the camp; but his young assistant,
Joshua son of Nun, would not leave the tent.
Exodus 33:11 NRSV

Now when Daniel knew that the writing was
signed, he went home. And in his upper room,
with his windows open toward Jerusalem,
he knelt down on his knees three times that day,
and prayed and gave thanks before his God,
as was his custom since early days.
Daniel 6:10 NKJV

Notes

9 Begin the Day with Prayer

The men who have done the most for God in this world have been early on their knees. He who fritters away the early morning, its opportunity and freshness, in other pursuits than seeking God will make poor headway seeking him the rest of the day. If God is not first in our thoughts and efforts in the morning, he will be in the last place the remainder of the day.

Behind this early rising and early praying is the ardent desire which presses us into this pursuit after God. Morning listlessness is the index to a listless heart. The heart which is behindhand in seeking God in the morning has lost its relish for God. David's heart was ardent after God. He hungered and thirsted after God, and so he sought God early, before daylight. The bed and sleep could not chain his soul in its eagerness after God. Christ longed for communion with God; and so, rising a great while before day, he would go out into the mountain to pray. The disciples, when fully awake and ashamed of their indulgence, would know where to find him. We might go through the list of men who have mightily impressed the world for God, and we would find them early after God.

A desire for God which cannot break the chains of sleep is a weak thing and will do but little good for God after it has indulged itself fully. The desire for God that keeps so far behind the devil and the world at the beginning of the day will never catch up.

It is not simply the getting up that puts men to the front and makes them captain generals in God's hosts, but it is the ardent desire which stirs and breaks all self-indulgent chains. But the getting up gives vent, increase, and strength to the desire. If they had lain in bed and indulged themselves, the desire would have been quenched. The desire aroused them and put them on the stretch for God, and this heeding and acting on the call gave their faith its grasp on God and gave to their hearts the sweetest and fullest revelation of God, and this strength of faith and fullness of revelation made them saints by eminence, and the halo of their sainthood has come down to us, and we have entered on the enjoyment of their conquests. But we take our fill in enjoyment, and not in productions. We build their tombs and write their epitaphs, but are careful not to follow their examples.

We need a generation of preachers who seek God and seek him early, who give the freshness and dew of effort to God, and secure in return the freshness and fullness of his power that he may be as the dew to them, full of gladness and strength, through all the heat and labour of the day. Our laziness after God is our crying sin. The children of this world are far wiser than we. They are at it early and late. We do not seek God with ardour and diligence. No man gets God who does not follow hard after him, and no soul follows hard after God who is not after him in early morn.

Reflect

How is your morning routine of prayer going? What can you do to strengthen it and make it more regular? Assess what is working well, and also what is unhelpful and could be done better. Make any adjustments that will help you to have a richer time of prayer.

Pray

Father God, thank You that it is You who gives restful sleep to those You love (Psalm 127:2). I receive the life of the Holy Spirit in my physical body. Strengthen me to keep seeking Your face in the early hours of my day. In Jesus' name I ask, amen.

Meditate

My voice You shall hear in the morning, O Lord;
In the morning I will direct it to You,
And I will look up.
Psalm 5:3 NKJV

In everything you do,
put God first, and he will direct you
and crown your efforts with success.
Proverbs 3:6 TLB

Notes

10 Prayer and Devotion United

Never was there greater need for saintly men and women; more imperative still is the call for saintly, God-devoted preachers. The world moves with gigantic strides. Satan has his hold and rule on the world, and labours to make all its movements subserve his ends. Religion must do its best work, present its most attractive and perfect models. By every means, modern sainthood must be inspired by the loftiest ideals and by the largest possibilities through the Spirit. Paul lived on his knees, that the Ephesian Church might measure the heights, breadths, and depths of an unmeasurable saintliness, and "be filled with all the fullness of God." Epaphras laid himself out with the exhaustive toil and strenuous conflict of fervent prayer, that the Colossian Church might "stand perfect and complete in all the will of God." Everywhere, everything in apostolic times was on the stretch that the people of God might each and "all come in the unity of the faith, and of the knowledge of the Son of God, unto a perfect man, unto the measure of the stature of the fullness of Christ." No premium was given to dwarfs; no encouragement to an old babyhood. The babies were to grow; the old, instead of feebleness and infirmities, were to bear fruit in old age, and be fat and flourishing. The divinest thing in religion is holy men and holy women.

No amount of money, genius, or culture can move things for God. Holiness energizing the soul, the whole man aflame with love, with desire for more faith, more prayer, more zeal, more consecration – this is the secret of power. These we need and must have, and men must be the incarnation of this God-inflamed devotedness. God's advance has been stayed, his cause crippled: his name dishonoured for their lack. Genius (though the loftiest and most gifted), education (though the most learned and refined), position, dignity, place, honoured names, high ecclesiastics cannot move this chariot of our God. It is a fiery one, and fiery forces only can move it. The genius of a Milton fails. The imperial strength of a Leo fails. Brainerd's spirit can move it. Brainerd's spirit was on fire for God, on fire for souls. Nothing earthly, worldly, selfish came in to abate in the least the intensity of this all-impelling and all-consuming force and flame.

Prayer is the creator as well as the channel of devotion. The spirit of devotion is the spirit of prayer. Prayer and devotion are united as soul and body are united, as life and the heart are united. There is no real prayer without devotion, no devotion without prayer. The preacher must be surrendered to God in the holiest devotion. He is not a professional man, his ministry is not a profession; it is a divine institution, a divine devotion. He is devoted to God. His aim, aspirations, ambition are for God and to God, and to such prayer is as essential as food is to life.

The preacher, above everything else, must be devoted to God. The preacher's relations to God are the insignia and credentials of his ministry. These must be clear, conclusive, unmistakable. No common, surface type of piety must be his. If he does not excel in grace, he does not excel at all. If he does not preach by life, character, conduct, he does not preach at all. If his piety be light, his preaching may be as soft and as sweet as music, as gifted as Apollo, yet its weight will be a feather's weight, visionary, fleeting as the morning cloud or the early dew. Devotion to God – there is no substitute for this in the preacher's character and conduct. Devotion to a Church, to opinions, to an organization, to orthodoxy – these are paltry, misleading, and vain when they become the source of inspiration, the animus of a call. God must be the mainspring of the preacher's effort, the fountain and crown of all his toil. The name and honour of Jesus Christ, the advance of his cause, must be all in all. The preacher must have no inspiration but the name of Jesus Christ, no ambition but to have him glorified, no toil but for him. Then prayer will be a source of his illuminations, the means of perpetual advance, the gauge of his success. The perpetual aim, the only ambition, the preacher can cherish is to have God with him.

Never did the cause of God need perfect illustrations of the possibilities of prayer more than in this age. No age, no person, will be ensamples of the gospel power except the ages or persons of deep and earnest prayer. A prayerless age will have but scant models of divine power. Prayerless hearts will never rise to these Alpine heights. The age may be a better age than the past, but there is an infinite distance between the betterment of an age by the force of an advancing civilization and its betterment by the increase of holiness and Christlikeness by the energy of prayer. The Jews were much better when Christ came than in the ages before. It was the golden age of their Pharisaic religion. Their golden religious age crucified Christ. Never more praying, never less praying; never more sacrifices, never less sacrifice; never less idolatry, never more idolatry; never more of temple worship, never less of God worship; never more of lip service, never less of heart service (God worshiped by lips whose hearts and hands crucified God's Son!); never more of churchgoers, never less of saints.

It is prayer-force which makes saints. Holy characters are formed by the power of real praying. The more of true saints, the more of praying; the more of praying, the more of true saints.

Reflect

How can you combine prayer with devotional reading and meditation to deepen your spiritual insights? Learn to pray-read the scriptures. This allows the scriptures to shape your prayer life. Perhaps use a devotional book and begin your time with the Lord by reading from that book.

Pray

Father God, I set aside every agenda as I seek Your face today. I say 'Yes' and 'Amen' to Your plans to do a deep work in my heart in the place of prayer. May the cry of my heart only be for more of Christ and His glory. In Jesus' name I ask, amen.

Meditate

Continue earnestly in prayer,
being vigilant in it with thanksgiving;
Colossians 4:2 NKJV

Yet indeed I also count all things loss for the
excellence of the knowledge of Christ Jesus
my Lord, for whom I have suffered
the loss of all things, and count them as rubbish,
that I may gain Christ and be found in Him,
not having my own righteousness, which is from
the law, but that which is through faith in Christ,
the righteousness which is from God by faith;
Philippians 3:8-9 NKJV

Notes

11 An Example of Devotion

God has now, and has had, many of these devoted, prayerful preachers – men in whose lives prayer has been a mighty, controlling, conspicuous force. The world has felt their power, God has felt and honoured their power, God's cause has moved mightily and swiftly by their prayers, holiness has shone out in their characters with a divine effulgence.

God found one of the men he was looking for in David Brainerd, whose work and name have gone into history. He was no ordinary man, but was capable of shining in any company, the peer of the wise and gifted ones, eminently suited to fill the most attractive pulpits and to labour among the most refined and the cultured, who were so anxious to secure him for their pastor. President Edwards bears testimony that he was "a young man of distinguished talents, had extraordinary knowledge of men and things, had rare conversational powers, excelled in his knowledge of theology, and was truly, for one so young, an extraordinary divine, and especially in all matters relating to experimental religion. I never knew his equal of his age and standing for clear and accurate notions of the nature and essence of true religion. His manner in prayer was almost inimitable, such as I have very rarely known equalled. His learning was very considerable, and he had extraordinary gifts for the pulpit."

No sublimer story has been recorded in earthly annals than that of David Brainerd; no miracle attests with diviner force the truth of Christianity than the life and work of such a man. Alone in the savage wilds of America, struggling day and night with a mortal disease, unschooled in the care of souls, having access to the Indians for a large portion of time only through the bungling medium of a pagan interpreter, with the Word of God in his heart and in his hand, his soul fired with the divine flame, a place and time to pour out his soul to God in prayer, he fully established the worship of God and secured all its gracious results. The Indians were changed with a great change from the lowest besotments of an ignorant and debased heathenism to pure, devout, intelligent Christians; all vice reformed, the external duties of Christianity at once embraced and acted on; family prayer set up; the Sabbath instituted and religiously observed; the internal graces of religion exhibited with growing sweetness and strength.

The solution of these results is found in David Brainerd himself, not in the conditions or accidents but in the man Brainerd. He was God's man, for God first and last and all the time. God could flow unhindered through him. The omnipotence of grace was neither arrested nor straightened by the conditions of his heart; the whole channel was broadened and cleaned out for God's fullest and most powerful passage, so that God with all his mighty forces could come down on the hopeless, savage wilderness, and transform it into his blooming and fruitful garden; for nothing is too hard for God to do if he can get the right kind of a man to do it with.

Brainerd lived the life of holiness and prayer. His diary is full and monotonous with the record of his seasons of fasting, meditation, and retirement. The time he spent in private prayer amounted to many hours daily. "When I return home," he said, "and give myself to meditation, prayer, and fasting, my soul longs for mortification, self-denial, humility, and divorcement from all things of the world." "I have nothing to do," he said, "with earth but only to labour in it honestly for God. I do not desire to live one minute for anything which earth can afford." After this high order did he pray: "Feeling somewhat of the sweetness of communion with God and the constraining force of his love, and how admirably it captivates the soul and makes all the desires and affections to centre in God, I set apart this day for secret fasting and prayer, to entreat God to direct and bless me with regard to the great work which I have in view of preaching the gospel, and that the Lord would return to me and show me the light of his countenance. I had little life and power in the forenoon. Near the middle of the afternoon God enabled me to wrestle ardently in intercession for my absent friends, but just at night the Lord visited me marvellously in prayer. I think my soul was never in such agony before. I felt no restraint, for the treasures of divine grace were opened to me. I wrestled for absent friends, for the ingathering of souls, for multitudes of poor souls, and for many that I thought were the children of God, personally, in many distant places. I was in such agony from sun half an hour high till near dark that I was all over wet with sweat, but yet it seemed to me I had done nothing. O, my dear Saviour did sweat blood for poor souls! I longed for more compassion toward them. I felt still in a sweet frame, under a sense of divine love and grace, and went to bed in such a frame, with my heart set on God." It was prayer which gave to his life and ministry their marvellous power.

The men of mighty prayer are men of spiritual might. Prayers never die. Brainerd's whole life was a life of prayer. By day and by night he prayed. Before preaching and after preaching he prayed. Riding through the interminable solitudes of the forests he prayed. On his bed of straw he prayed. Retiring to the dense and lonely forests, he prayed. Hour by hour, day after day, early morn and late at night, he was praying and fasting, pouring out his soul, interceding, communing with God. He was with God mightily in prayer, and God was with him mightily, and by it he being dead yet speaketh and worketh, and will speak and work till the end comes, and among the glorious ones of that glorious day he will be with the first.

Jonathan Edwards says of him: "His life shows the right way to success in the works of the ministry. He sought it as the soldier seeks victory in a siege or battle; or as a man that runs a race for a great prize. Animated with love to Christ and souls, how did he labour? Always fervently. Not only in word and doctrine, in public and in private, but in prayers by day and night, wrestling with God in secret and travailing in birth with unutterable groans and agonies, until Christ was formed in the hearts of the people to whom he was sent. Like a true son of Jacob, he persevered in wrestling through all the darkness of the night, until the breaking of the day!"

Reflect

What is one practice of someone who has prioritised prayer above all else in his or her life, that you can emulate? You don't have to copy it exactly but it can serve as an inspiration for doing something similar. You could also have a conversation with someone you admire for their prayer life and ask them to give you any wisdom that would help you.

Pray

Father God, show me how I may better prioritise prayer time spent with You, over every other thing in my life. Burn away anything in me that resists or hinders Your work in and through me. In Jesus' name I ask, amen.

Meditate

Now it came to pass in those days
that He went out to the mountain to pray,
and continued all night in prayer to God.
Luke 6:12 NKJV

Elijah was a man with a nature like ours,
and he prayed earnestly that it would not rain;
and it did not rain on the land
for three years and six months.
James 5:17 NKJV

Notes

12 Heart Preparation Necessary

Prayer, with its manifold and many-sided forces, helps the mouth to utter the truth in its fullness and freedom. The preacher is to be prayed for, the preacher is made by prayer. The preacher's mouth is to be prayed for; his mouth is to be opened and filled by prayer. A holy mouth is made by praying, by much praying; a brave mouth is made by praying, by much praying. The Church and the world, God and heaven, owe much to Paul's mouth; Paul's mouth owed its power to prayer.

How manifold, illimitable, valuable, and helpful prayer is to the preacher in so many ways, at so many points, in every way! One great value is, it helps his heart.

Praying makes the preacher a heart preacher. Prayer puts the preacher's heart into the preacher's sermon; prayer puts the preacher's sermon into the preacher's heart.

The heart makes the preacher. Men of great hearts are great preachers. Men of bad hearts may do a measure of good, but this is rare. The hireling and the stranger may help the sheep at some points, but it is the good shepherd with the good shepherd's heart who will bless the sheep and answer the full measure of the shepherd's place.

We have emphasized sermon-preparation until we have lost sight of the important thing to be prepared – the heart. A prepared heart is much better than a prepared sermon. A prepared heart will make a prepared sermon.

Volumes have been written laying down the mechanics and taste of sermon-making, until we have become possessed with the idea that this scaffolding is the building. The young preacher has been taught to lay out all his strength on the form, taste, and beauty of his sermon as a mechanical and intellectual product. We have thereby cultivated a vicious taste among the people and raised the clamour for talent instead of grace, eloquence instead of piety, rhetoric instead of revelation, reputation and brilliancy instead of holiness. By it we have lost the true idea of preaching, lost preaching power, lost pungent conviction for sin, lost the rich experience and elevated Christian character, lost the authority over consciences and lives which always results from genuine preaching.

It would not do to say that preachers study too much. Some of them do not study at all; others do not study enough. Numbers do not study the right way to show themselves workmen approved of God. But our great lack is not in head culture, but in heart culture; not lack of knowledge but lack of holiness is our sad and telling defect – not that we know too much, but that we do not meditate on God and his word and watch and fast and pray enough. The heart is the great hindrance to our preaching. Words pregnant with divine truth find in our hearts non-conductors; arrested, they fall shorn and powerless.

Can ambition, that lusts after praise and place, preach the gospel of Him who made himself of no reputation and took on Him the form of a servant? Can the proud, the vain, the egotistical preach the gospel of him who was meek and lowly? Can the bad-tempered, passionate, selfish, hard, worldly man preach the system which teems with long-suffering, self-denial, tenderness, which imperatively demands separation from enmity and crucifixion to the world? Can the hireling official, heartless, perfunctory, preach the gospel which demands the shepherd to give his life for the sheep? Can the covetous man, who counts salary and money, preach the gospel till he has gleaned his heart and can say in the spirit of Christ and Paul in the words of Wesley: "I count it dung and dross; I trample it under my feet; I (yet not I, but the grace of God in me) esteem it just as the mire of the streets, I desire it not, I seek it not?" God's revelation does not need the light of human genius, the polish and strength of human culture, the brilliancy of human thought, the force of human brains to adorn or enforce it; but it does demand the simplicity, the docility, humility, and faith of a child's heart.

It was this surrender and subordination of intellect and genius to the divine and spiritual forces which made Paul peerless among the apostles. It was this which gave Wesley his power and radicated his labours in the history of humanity. This gave to Loyola the strength to arrest the retreating forces of Catholicism.

Our great need is heart-preparation. Luther held it as an axiom: "He who has prayed well has studied well." We do not say that men are not to think and use their intellects; but he will use his intellect best who cultivates his heart most. We do not say that preachers should not be students; but we do say that their great study should be the Bible, and he studies the Bible best who has kept his heart with diligence. We do not say that the preacher should not know men, but he will be the greater adept in human nature who has fathomed the depths and intricacies of his own heart. We do say that while the channel of preaching is the mind, its fountain is the heart; you may broaden and deepen the channel, but if you do not look well to the purity and depth of the fountain, you will have a dry or polluted channel. We do say that almost any man of common intelligence has sense enough to preach the gospel, but very few have grace enough to do so. We do say that he who has struggled with his own heart and conquered it; who has taught it humility, faith, love, truth, mercy, sympathy, courage; who can pour the rich treasures of the heart thus trained, through a manly intellect, all surcharged with the power of the gospel on the consciences of his hearers – such a one will be the truest, most successful preacher in the esteem of his Lord.

Reflect

How will you prepare your heart before praying, ensuring it is free from distractions and focused on God? Consider the following key points:

- Make sure there is no unforgiveness in your heart.
- Give the Lord any cares or burdens that are troubling you.
- Praise and thanksgiving are good to clear the spiritual atmosphere.

Pray

Father God, unite my heart to fear Your name (Psalm 86:11). Be my support and refuge as You deal with the hidden issues of my heart. I surrender my thoughts, opinions, desires and emotions to Your merciful hands. In Jesus' name I ask, amen.

Meditate

If I regard iniquity in my heart,
the Lord will not hear.
Psalm 66:18 NKJV

Above all else, guard your heart,
for everything you do flows from it.
Proverbs 4:23 NIV

Notes

13 Grace from the Heart Rather than the Head

The heart is the Saviour of the world. Heads do not save. Genius, brains, brilliancy, strength, natural gifts do not save. The gospel flows through hearts. All the mightiest forces are heart forces. All the sweetest and loveliest graces are heart graces. Great hearts make great characters; great hearts make divine characters. God is love. There is nothing greater than love, nothing greater than God. Hearts make heaven; heaven is love. There is nothing higher, nothing sweeter, than heaven. It is the heart and not the head which makes God's great preachers. The heart counts much every way in religion. The heart must speak from the pulpit. The heart must hear in the pew. In fact, we serve God with our hearts. Head homage does not pass current in heaven.

We believe that one of the serious and most popular errors of the modern pulpit is the putting of more thought than prayer, of more head than of heart in its sermons. Big hearts make big preachers; good hearts make good preachers. A theological school to enlarge and cultivate the heart is the golden desideratum of the gospel. The pastor binds his people to him and rules his people by his heart. They may admire his gifts, they may be proud of his ability, they may be affected for the time by his sermons; but the stronghold of his power is his heart. His sceptre is love. The throne of his power is his heart.

The good shepherd gives his life for the sheep. Heads never make martyrs. It is the heart which surrenders the life to love and fidelity. It takes great courage to be a faithful pastor, but the heart alone can supply this courage. Gifts and genius may be brave, but it is the gifts and genius of the heart and not of the head.

It is easier to fill the head than it is to prepare the heart. It is easier to make a brain sermon than a heart sermon. It was heart that drew the Son of God from heaven. It is heart that will draw men to heaven. Men of heart is what the world needs to sympathize with its woe, to kiss away its sorrows, to compassionate its misery, and to alleviate its pain. Christ was eminently the man of sorrows, because he was pre-eminently the man of heart.

"Give me thy heart," is God's requisition of men. "Give me thy heart! is man's demand of man.

A professional ministry is a heartless ministry. When salary plays a great part in the ministry, the heart plays little part. We may make preaching our business, and not put our hearts in the business. He who puts self to the front in his preaching puts heart to the rear. He who does not sow with his heart in his study will never reap a harvest for God. The closet is the heart's study. We will learn more about how to preach and what to preach there than we can learn in our libraries. "Jesus wept" is the shortest and biggest verse in the Bible. It is he who goes forth weeping (not preaching great sermons), bearing precious seed, who shall come again rejoicing, bringing his sheaves with him.

Praying gives sense, brings wisdom, broadens and strengthens the mind. The closet is a perfect schoolteacher and schoolhouse for the preacher. Thought is not only brightened and clarified in prayer, but thought is born in prayer. We can learn more in an hour praying, when praying indeed, than from many hours in the study. Books are in the closet which can be found and read nowhere else. Revelations are made in the closet which are made nowhere else.

Reflect

How can you ensure your prayers flow from a heart full of grace and love, rather than being a mere intellectual exercise? Think about keeping it relational, not formal. Take time to breathe and acknowledge that the Lord is present and this is a conversation you are having with a loving Father.

Pray

Father God, help me put heart and head in the right order, both in my relationship with You and with others. I know I have been set free and empowered to obey You - help me to live this out with a whole and healthy heart in every area of my life. In Jesus' name I ask, amen.

Meditate

Praying always with all prayer and supplication
in the Spirit, being watchful to this end
with all perseverance and supplication
for all the saints.
Ephesians 6:18 NKJV

The Lord says: "These people come near to me
with their mouth and honour me with their lips,
but their hearts are far from me. Their worship
of me is based on merely human rules
they have been taught."
Isaiah 29:13 NIV

If I speak in the tongues of mortals and of angels,
but do not have love, I am a noisy gong or a
clanging cymbal. And if I have prophetic powers,
and understand all mysteries and all knowledge,
and if I have all faith, so as to remove mountains,
but do not have love, I am nothing.
1 Corinthians 13:1-2 NRSV

Notes

14 Unction a Necessity

Alexander Knox, a Christian philosopher of the days of Wesley, not an adherent but a strong personal friend of Wesley, and with much spiritual sympathy with the Wesleyan movement, writes: "It is strange and lamentable, but I verily believe the fact to be that except among Methodists and Methodistical clergyman, there is not much interesting preaching in England. The clergy, too generally have absolutely lost the art. There is, I conceive, in the great laws of the moral world a kind of secret understanding like the affinities in chemistry, between rightly promulgated religious truth and the deepest feelings of the human mind. Where the one is duly exhibited, the other will respond. Did not our hearts burn within us? – but to this devout feeling is indispensable in the speaker.

Now, I am obliged to state from my own observation that this unction, as the French not unfitly term it, is beyond all comparison more likely to be found in England in a Methodist conventicle than in a parish Church. This, and this alone, seems really to be that which fills the Methodist houses and thins the Churches. I am, I verily think, no enthusiast; I am a most sincere and cordial churchman, a humble disciple of the School of Hale and Boyle, of Burnet and Leighton. Now I must aver that when I was in this country, two years ago, I did not hear a single preacher who taught me like my own great masters but such as are deemed Methodistical. And I now despair of getting an atom of heart instruction from any other quarter. The Methodist preachers (however I may not always approve of all their expressions) do most assuredly diffuse this true religion and undefiled. I felt real pleasure last Sunday. I can bear witness that the preacher did at once speak the words of truth and soberness. There was no eloquence – the honest man never dreamed of such a thing but there was far better: a cordial communication of vitalized truth. I say vitalized because what he declared to others it was impossible not to feel he lived on himself."

This unction is the art of preaching. The preacher who never had this unction never had the art of preaching. The preacher who has lost this unction has lost the art of preaching. Whatever other arts he may have and retain the art of sermon-making, the art of eloquence, the art of great, clear thinking, the art of pleasing an audience he has lost the divine art of preaching. This unction makes God's truth powerful and interesting, draws and attracts, edifies, convicts, saves.

This unction vitalizes God's revealed truth, makes it living and life-giving. Even God's truth spoken without this unction is light, dead, and deadening. Though abounding in truth, though weighty with thought, though sparkling with rhetoric, though pointed by logic, though powerful by earnestness, without this divine unction it issues in death and not in life. Mr. Spurgeon says: "I wonder how long we might beat our brains before we could plainly put into word what is meant by preaching with unction. Yet he who preaches knows its presence, and he who hears soon detects its absence. Samaria, in famine, typifies a discourse without it. Jerusalem, with her feast of fat things, full of marrow, may represent a sermon enriched with it. Everyone knows what the freshness of the morning is when orient pearls abound on every blade of grass, but who can describe it, much less produce it of itself? Such is the mystery of spiritual anointing. We know, but we cannot tell to others what it is. It is as easy as it is foolish, to counterfeit it. Unction is a thing which you cannot manufacture, and its counterfeits are worse than worthless. Yet it is, in itself, priceless, and beyond measure needful if you would edify believers and bring sinners to Christ."

Reflect

- What is one thing you can do to grow in the anointing of the Holy Spirit in your prayers?
- Do you depend more on head preparation rather than the heart? Think through whether you give more time to the practical preparation rather than the spiritual? How can you change that?
- Pray for the people you lead or minister too.

Pray

Father God, thank You that I can live out the Kingdom of God here and now. Please continue to bring alignment to all areas of my life so that my life itself preaches Your message and ushers in Your presence. In Jesus' name I ask, amen.

Meditate

"If you then, being evil, know how to give good gifts to your children, how much more will your heavenly Father give the Holy Spirit to those who ask Him!"

Luke 11:13 NKJV

Do not merely listen to the word, and so deceive yourselves. Do what it says.

James 1:22 NIV

Since we live by the Spirit, let us keep in step with the Spirit.

Galatians 5:25 NIV

Notes

15 Unction, the Mark of True Gospel Preaching

Unction is that indefinable, indescribable something which an old, renowned Scotch preacher describes thus: "There is sometimes somewhat in preaching that cannot be ascribed either to matter or expression, and cannot be described what it is, or from whence it cometh, but with a sweet violence it pierceth into the heart and affections and comes immediately from the Word; but if there be any way to obtain such a thing, it is by the heavenly disposition of the speaker."

We call it unction. It is this unction which makes the word of God "quick and powerful, and sharper than any two-edged sword, piercing even to the dividing asunder of soul and spirit, and of the joints and marrow, and a discerner of the thoughts and intents of the heart." It is this unction which gives the words of the preacher such point, sharpness, and power, and which creates such friction and stir in many a dead congregation. The same truths have been told in the strictness of the letter, smooth as human oil could make them; but no signs of life, not a pulse throb; all as peaceful as the grave and as dead. The same preacher in the meanwhile receives a baptism of this unction, the divine inflatus is on him, the letter of the Word has been embellished and fired by this mysterious power, and the throbbings of life begin –

life which receives or life which resists. The unction pervades and convicts the conscience and breaks the heart.

This divine unction is the feature which separates and distinguishes true gospel preaching from all other methods of presenting the truth, and which creates a wide spiritual chasm between the preacher who has it and the one who has it not. It backs and impregnates revealed truth with all the energy of God. Unction is simply putting God in his own word and on his own preachers. By mighty and great prayerfulness and by continual prayerfulness, it is all potential and personal to the preacher; it inspires and clarifies his intellect, gives insight and grasp and projecting power; it gives to the preacher heart power, which is greater than head power; and tenderness, purity, force flow from the heart by it. Enlargement, freedom, fullness of thought, directness and simplicity of utterance are the fruits of this unction.

Often earnestness is mistaken for this unction. He who has the divine unction will be earnest in the very spiritual nature of things, but there may be a vast deal of earnestness without the least mixture of unction.

Earnestness and unction look alike from some points of view. Earnestness may be readily and without detection substituted or mistaken for unction. It requires a spiritual eye and a spiritual taste to discriminate.

Earnestness may be sincere, serious, ardent, and persevering. It goes at a thing with good will, pursues it with perseverance, and urges it with ardour; puts force in it. But all these forces do not rise higher than the mere human. The man is in it – the whole man, with all that he has of will and heart, of brain and genius, of planning and working and talking. He has set himself to some purpose which has mastered him, and he pursues to master it. There may be none of God in it. There may be little of God in it, because there is so much of the man in it. He may present pleas in advocacy of his earnest purpose which please or touch and move or overwhelm with conviction of their importance; and in all this earnestness may move along earthly ways, being propelled by human forces only, its altar made by earthly hands and its fire kindled by earthly flames. It is said of a rather famous preacher of gifts, whose construction of Scripture was to his fancy or purpose, that he "grew very eloquent over his own exegesis." So men grow exceeding earnest over their own plans or movements. Earnestness may be selfishness simulated.

What of unction? It is the indefinable in preaching which makes it preaching. It is that which distinguishes and separates preaching from all mere human addresses. It is the divine in preaching. It makes the preaching sharp to those who need sharpness. It distils as the dew to those who need to be refreshed. It is well described as:

"a two-edged sword
Of heavenly temper keen,
And double were the wounds it made
Wherever it glanced between.
'Twas death to silt; 'twas life
To all who mourned for sin.
It kindled and it silenced strife,
Made war and peace within."

This unction comes to the preacher not in the study but in the closet. It is heaven's distillation in answer to prayer. It is the sweetest exhalation of the Holy Spirit. It impregnates, suffuses, softens, percolates, cuts, and soothes. It carries the Word like dynamite, like salt, like sugar; makes the Word a soother, an arranger, a revealer, a searcher; makes the hearer a culprit or a saint, makes him weep like a child and live like a giant; opens his heart and his purse as gently, yet as strongly as the spring opens the leaves. This unction is not the gift of genius. It is not found in the halls of learning. No eloquence can woo it. No industry can win it. No prelatical hands can confer it. It is the gift of God – the signet set to his own messengers. It is heaven's knighthood given to the chosen true and brave ones who have sought this anointed honour through many an hour of tearful, wrestling prayer.

Earnestness is good and impressive: genius is gifted and great. Thought kindles and inspires, but it takes a diviner endowment, a more powerful energy than earnestness or genius or thought to break the chains of sin, to win estranged and depraved hearts to God, to repair the breaches and restore the Church to her old ways of purity and power. Nothing but this holy unction can do this.

Reflect

- ❖ How will you ensure that your preaching or leadership are empowered by prayer and the Holy Spirit? Praying in tongues could help – Paul said he prayed in tongues more than all the Corinthians (1 Corinthians 14:18).
- ❖ A life of purity in thought, word and deed increases one's anointing. Is there anything contaminating your life that you need to turn away from?

Pray

Father God, please set a guard over my mouth and consecrate my tongue. I resolve to perform only for You and not to men. Help me to grow in obedience to Your leading so that I only speak what You give. In Jesus' name I ask, amen.

Meditate

But you have an anointing from the Holy One,
and all of you know the truth.
1 John 2:20 NIV

And so it was with me, brothers and sisters.
When I came to you, I did not come with
eloquence or human wisdom
as I proclaimed to you the testimony about God.
For I resolved to know nothing
while I was with you except Jesus Christ
and him crucified.
1 Corinthians 2:1-2 NIV

But, 'Let the one who boasts boast in the Lord.'
For it is not the one who commends himself
who is approved,
but the one whom the Lord commends.
2 Corinthians 10:17-18 NIV

Notes

16 Much Prayer the Price of Unction

In the Christian system unction is the anointing of the Holy Ghost, separating unto God's work and qualifying for it. This unction is the one divine enablement by which the preacher accomplishes the peculiar and saving ends of preaching. Without this unction there are no true spiritual results accomplished; the results and forces in preaching do not rise above the results of unsanctified speech. Without unction the former is as potent as the pulpit.

This divine unction on the preacher generates through the Word of God the spiritual results that flow from the gospel; and without this unction, these results are not secured. Many pleasant impressions may be made, but these all fall far below the ends of gospel preaching. This unction may be simulated. There are many things that look like it, there are many results that resemble its effects; but they are foreign to its results and to its nature. The fervour or softness excited by a pathetic or emotional sermon may look like the movements of the divine unction, but they have no pungent, perpetrating heart-breaking force. No heart-healing balm is there in these surface, sympathetic, emotional movements; they are not radical, neither sin-searching nor sin-curing.

This divine unction is the one distinguishing feature that separates true gospel preaching from all other methods of presenting truth. It backs and interpenetrates the revealed truth with all the force of God. It illumines the Word and broadens and enrichens the intellect and empowers it to grasp and apprehend the Word. It qualifies the preacher's heart, and brings it to that condition of tenderness, of purity, of force and light that are necessary to secure the highest results. This unction gives to the preacher liberty and enlargement of thought and soul – a freedom, fullness, and directness of utterance that can be secured by no other process.

Without this unction on the preacher the gospel has no more power to propagate itself than any other system of truth. This is the seal of its divinity. Unction in the preacher puts God in the gospel. Without the unction, God is absent, and the gospel is left to the low and unsatisfactory forces that the ingenuity, interest, or talents of men can devise to enforce and project its doctrines.

It is in this element that the pulpit oftener fails than in any other element. Just at this all-important point it lapses. Learning it may have, brilliancy and eloquence may delight and charm, sensation or less offensive methods may bring the populace in crowds, mental power may impress and enforce truth with all its resources; but without this unction, each and all these will be but as the fretful assault of the waters on a

Gibraltar. Spray and foam may cover and spangle; but the rocks are there still, unimpressed and unimpressible. The human heart can no more be swept of its hardness and sin by these human forces than these rocks can be swept away by the ocean's ceaseless flow.

This unction is the consecration force, and its presence the continuous test of that consecration. It is this divine anointing on the preacher that secures his consecration to God and his work. Other forces and motives may call him to the work, but this only is consecration. A separation to God's work by the power of the Holy Spirit is the only consecration recognized by God as legitimate.

The unction, the divine unction, this heavenly anointing, is what the pulpit needs and must have. This divine and heavenly oil put on it by the imposition of God's hand must soften and lubricate the whole man – heart, head, spirit – until it separates him with a mighty separation from all earthly, secular, worldly, selfish motives and aims, separating him to everything that is pure and Godlike.

It is the presence of this unction on the preacher that creates the stir and friction in many a congregation. The same truths have been told in the strictness of the letter, but no ruffle has been seen, no pain or pulsation felt. All is quiet as a graveyard. Another preacher comes, and this mysterious influence is on him; the letter of the Word has been fired by the Spirit, the throes of a mighty movement are felt, it is the unction that pervades and stirs the conscience and breaks the heart. Unctionless preaching makes everything hard, dry, acrid, dead.

This unction is not a memory or an era of the past only; it is a present, realized, conscious fact. It belongs to the experience of the man as well as to his preaching. It is that which transforms him into the image of his divine Master, as well as that by which he declares the truths of Christ with power. It is so much the power in the ministry as to make all else seem feeble and vain without it, and by its presence to atone for the absence of all other and feebler forces.

This unction is not an inalienable gift. It is a conditional gift, and its presence is perpetuated and increased by the same process by which it was at first secured; by unceasing prayer to God, by impassioned desires after God, by estimating it, by seeking it with tireless ardour, by deeming all else loss and failure without it.

How and whence comes this unction? Direct from God in answer to prayer. Praying hearts only are the hearts filled with this holy oil; praying lips only are anointed with this divine unction.

Prayer, much prayer, is the price of preaching unction; prayer, much prayer, is the one, sole condition of keeping this unction. Without unceasing prayer the unction never comes to the preacher. Without perseverance in prayer, the unction, like the manna overkept, breeds worms.

Reflect

Think of one way to free up time to give yourself to a life saturated in prayer. This might be forgoing a TV programme or spending less time on social media. How about beginning to fast one day a week?

Pray

Father God, I dedicate my lips and heart to pray Your words and what is in Your heart. Help me to dedicate the hours of my day to You so I can truly learn to pray without ceasing. In Jesus' name I ask, amen.

Meditate

"...but we will give ourselves continually to prayer and to the ministry of the word."
Acts 6:4 NKJV

To these four young men God gave knowledge and understanding of all kinds of literature and learning. And Daniel could understand visions and dreams of all kinds.
Daniel 1:17 NIV

It shall come to pass in that day
That his burden will be taken away from your shoulder, And his yoke from your neck,
And the yoke will be destroyed
because of the anointing oil.
Isaiah 10:27 NKJV

Notes

17 Prayer Marks Spiritual Leadership

The apostles knew the necessity and worth of prayer to their ministry. They knew that their high commission as apostles, instead of relieving them from the necessity of prayer, committed them to it by a more urgent need; so that they were exceedingly jealous else some other important work should exhaust their time and prevent their praying as they ought; so they appointed laymen to look after the delicate and engrossing duties of ministering to the poor, that they (the apostles) might, unhindered, "give themselves continually to prayer and to the ministry of the word." Prayer is put first, and their relation to prayer is put most strongly – "give themselves to it," making a business of it, surrendering themselves to praying, putting fervour, urgency, perseverance, and time in it.

How holy, apostolic men devoted themselves to this divine work of prayer! "Night and day praying exceedingly," says Paul. "We will give ourselves continually to prayer" is the consensus of apostolic devotement. How these New Testament preachers laid themselves out in prayer for God's people! How they put God in full force into their Churches by their praying! These holy apostles did not vainly fancy that they had met their high and solemn duties by delivering faithfully God's word, but their preaching was made to stick and tell by the ardour and insistence of their praying. Apostolic praying was as taxing, toilsome, and imperative as apostolic preaching. They prayed mightily day and night to bring their people to the highest regions of faith and holiness. They prayed mightier still to hold them to this high spiritual altitude. The preacher who has never learned in the school of Christ the high and divine art of intercession for his people will never learn the art of preaching, though homiletics be poured into him by the ton, and though he be the most gifted genius in sermon-making and sermon-delivery.

The prayers of apostolic, saintly leaders do much in making saints of those who are not apostles. If the Church leaders in after years had been as particular and fervent in praying for their people as the apostles were, the sad, dark times of worldliness and apostasy had not marred the history and eclipsed the glory and arrested the advance of the Church. Apostolic praying makes apostolic saints and keeps apostolic times of purity and power in the Church.

What loftiness of soul, what purity and elevation of motive, what unselfishness, what self-sacrifice, what exhaustive toil, what ardour of spirit, what divine tact are requisite to be an intercessor for men!

The preacher is to lay himself out in prayer for his people; not that they might be saved, simply, but that they be mightily saved. The apostles laid themselves out in prayer that their saints might be perfect; not that they should have a little relish for the things of God, but that they "might be filled with all the fullness of God."

Paul did not rely on his apostolic preaching to secure this end, but "for this cause he bowed his knees to the Father of our Lord Jesus Christ."

Paul's praying carried Paul's converts farther along the highway of sainthood than Paul's preaching did. Epaphras did as much or more by prayer for the Colossian saints than by his preaching. He laboured fervently always in prayer for them that "they might stand perfect and complete in all the will of God."

Preachers are pre-eminently God's leaders. They are primarily responsible for the condition of the Church. They shape its character, give tone and direction to its life.

Much every way depends on these leaders. They shape the times and the institutions. The Church is divine, the treasure it encases is heavenly, but it bears the imprint of the human. The treasure is in earthen vessels, and it smacks of the vessel. The Church of God makes, or is made by, its leaders. Whether it makes them or is made by them, it will be what its leaders are; spiritual if they are so, secular if they are, conglomerate if its leaders are. Israel's kings gave character to Israel's piety. A Church rarely revolts against or rises above the religion of its leaders. Strongly spiritual leaders; men of holy might, at the lead, are tokens of God's favour; disaster and weakness follow the wake of feeble or worldly leaders. Israel had fallen low when God gave children to be their princes and babes to rule over them. No happy state is predicted by the prophets when children oppress God's Israel and women rule over them. Times of spiritual leadership are times of great spiritual prosperity to the Church.

Prayer is one of the eminent characteristics of strong spiritual leadership. Men of mighty prayer are men of might and mould things. Their power with God has the conquering tread.

How can a man preach who does not get his message fresh from God in the closet? How can he preach without having his faith quickened, his vision cleared, and his heart warmed by his closeting with God? Alas, for the pulpit lips which are untouched by this closet flame. Dry and unctionless they will ever be, and truths divine will never come with power from such lips. As far as the real interests of religion are concerned, a pulpit without a closet will always be a barren thing.

A preacher may preach in an official, entertaining, or learned way without prayer, but between this kind of preaching and sowing God's precious seed with holy hands and prayerful, weeping hearts there is an immeasurable distance.

A prayerless ministry is the undertaker for all God's truth and for God's Church. He may have the most costly casket and the most beautiful flowers, but it is a funeral, notwithstanding the charmful array. A prayerless Christian will never learn God's truth; a prayerless ministry will never be able to teach God's truth. Ages of millennial glory have been lost by a prayerless Church. The coming of our Lord has been postponed indefinitely by a prayerless Church. Hell has enlarged herself and filled her dire caves in the presence of the dead service of a prayerless Church.

The best, the greatest offering is an offering of prayer. If the preachers of the twentieth century will learn well the lesson of prayer, and use fully the power of prayer, the millennium will come to its noon ere the century closes. "Pray without ceasing" is the trumpet call to the preachers of the twentieth century. If the twentieth century will get their texts, their thoughts, their words, their sermons in their closets, the next century will find a new heaven and a new earth. The old sin-stained and sin-eclipsed heaven and earth will pass away under the power of a praying ministry.

Reflect

- Would you say that prayer is a defining part of your life?
- How can you lead by example in prayer?
- Are there a handful of people you could meet with weekly to pray for an hour?
- Could you commit to pray more faithfully before making decisions?

Pray

Father God, I make myself available to You in the building up of Your Church into a house of prayer. Show me how I might bring others along with me to live a life of deeper prayer and consecration, and lead me to the right people. In Jesus' name I ask, amen.

Meditate

"If My people who are called by My name will
humble themselves, and pray and seek My face,
and turn from their wicked ways,
then I will hear from heaven, and will forgive their
sin and heal their land."
2 Chronicles 7:14 NKJV

My dear children, for whom I am again in the
pains of childbirth until Christ is formed in you,
Galatians 4:19 NIV

"Yet I hold this against you:
You have forsaken the love you had at first.
Consider how far you have fallen! Repent and do
the things you did at first. If you do not repent,
I will come to you and remove your lampstand
from its place."
Revelations 2:4-5 NIV

Notes

18 Preachers Need the Prayers of the People

Somehow the practice of praying in particular for the preacher has fallen into disuse or become discounted. Occasionally have we heard the practice arraigned as a disparagement of the ministry, being a public declaration by those who do it of the inefficiency of the ministry. It offends the pride of learning and self-sufficiency, perhaps, and these ought to be offended and rebuked in a ministry that is so derelict as to allow them to exist.

Prayer, to the preacher, is not simply the duty of his profession, a privilege, but it is a necessity. Air is not more necessary to the lungs than prayer is to the preacher. It is absolutely necessary for the preacher to pray. It is an absolute necessity that the preacher be prayed for. These two propositions are wedded into a union which ought never to know any divorce: the preacher must pray; the preacher must be prayed for. It will take all the praying he can do, and all the praying he can get done, to meet the fearful responsibilities and gain the largest, truest success in his great work. The true preacher, next to the cultivation of the spirit and fact of prayer in himself, in their intensest form, covets with a great covetousness the prayers of God's people.

The holier a man is, the more does he estimate prayer; the clearer does he see that God gives himself to the praying ones, and that the measure of God's revelation to the soul is the measure of the soul's longing, importunate prayer for God. Salvation never finds its way to a prayerless heart. The Holy Spirit never abides in a prayerless spirit. Preaching never edifies a prayerless soul. Christ knows nothing of prayerless Christians. The gospel cannot be projected by a prayerless preacher. Gifts, talents, education, eloquence, God's call, cannot abate the demand of prayer, but only intensify the necessity for the preacher to pray and to be prayed for. The more the preacher's eyes are opened to the nature, responsibility, and difficulties in his work, the more will he see, and if he be a true preacher the more will he feel, the necessity of prayer; not only the increasing demand to pray himself, but to call on others to help him by their prayers.

Paul is an illustration of this. If any man could project the gospel by dint of personal force, by brain power, by culture, by personal grace, by God's apostolic commission, God's extraordinary call, that man was Paul. That the preacher must be a man given to prayer, Paul is an eminent example. That the true apostolic preacher must have the prayers of other good people to give to his ministry its full quota of success, Paul is a preeminent example. He asks, he covets, he pleads in an impassioned way for the help of all God's saints. He knew that in the spiritual realm, as elsewhere, in union there is strength; that the concentration and aggregation of faith, desire, and prayer increased the volume of spiritual force until it became overwhelming and irresistible in its power. Units of prayer combined, like drops of water, make an ocean which defies resistance. So Paul, with his clear and full apprehension of spiritual dynamics, determined to make his ministry as impressive, as eternal, as irresistible as the ocean, by gathering all the scattered units of prayer and precipitating them on his ministry. May not the solution of Paul's pre-eminence in labours and results, and impress on the Church and the world, be found in this fact that he was able to centre on himself and his ministry more of prayer than others?

To his brethren at Rome he wrote: "Now I beseech you, brethren, for the Lord Jesus Christ's sake, and for the love of the Spirit, that ye strive together with me in prayers to God for me." To the Ephesians he says: "Praying always with all prayer and supplication in the Spirit, and watching thereunto with all perseverance and supplication for all saints; and for me, that utterance may be given unto me, that I may open my mouth boldly, to make known the mystery of the gospel." To the Colossians he emphasizes: "Withal praying also for us, that God would open unto us a door of utterance, to speak the mystery of Christ, for which I am also in bonds: that I may make it manifest as I ought to speak." To the Thessalonians he says sharply, strongly: "Brethren, pray for us." Paul calls on the Corinthian Church to help him: "Ye also helping together by prayer for us." This was to be part of their work. They were to lay to the helping hand of prayer.

He in an additional and closing charge to the Thessalonian Church about the importance and necessity of their prayers says: "Finally, brethren, pray for us, that the word of the Lord may have free course, and be glorified, even as it is with you: and that we may be delivered from unreasonable and wicked men." He impresses the Philippians that all his trials and opposition can be made subservient to the spread of the gospel by the efficiency of their prayers for him. Philemon was to prepare a lodging for him, for through Philemon's prayer Paul was to be his guest.

Paul's attitude on this question illustrates his humility and his deep insight into the spiritual forces which project the gospel. More than this, it teaches a lesson for all times, that if Paul was so dependent on the prayers of God's saints to give his ministry success, how much greater the necessity that the prayers of God's saints be centred on the ministry of today!

Paul did not feel that this urgent plea for prayer was to lower his dignity, lessen his influence, or depreciate his piety. What if it did? Let dignity go, let influence be destroyed, let his reputation be marred – he must have their prayers. Called, commissioned, chief of the Apostles as he was, all his equipment was imperfect without the prayers of his people. He wrote letters everywhere, urging them to pray for him. Do you pray for your preacher? Do you pray for him in secret? Public prayers are of little worth unless they are founded on or followed up by private praying. The praying ones are to the preacher as Aaron and Hur were to Moses. They hold up his hands and decide the issue that is so fiercely raging around them.

The plea and purpose of the apostles were to put the Church to praying. They did not ignore the grace of cheerful giving. They were not ignorant of the place which religious activity and work occupied in the spiritual life; but not one nor all of these, in apostolic estimate or urgency, could at all compare in necessity and importance with prayer. The most sacred and urgent pleas were used, the most fervid exhortations, the most comprehensive and arousing words were uttered to enforce the all-important obligation and necessity of prayer.

"Put the saints everywhere to praying" is the burden of the apostolic effort and the keynote of apostolic success. Jesus Christ had striven to do this in the days of his personal ministry. As he was moved by infinite compassion at the ripened fields of earth perishing for lack of labourers and pausing in his own praying – he tries to awaken the stupid sensibilities of his disciples to the duty of prayer as he charges them, "Pray ye the Lord of the harvest that he will send forth labourers into his harvest." "And he spoke a parable unto them to this end, that men ought always to pray and not to faint."

Reflect

- ❖ How can you encourage your congregation to pray biblically for their leaders?
- ❖ Will you commit to pray daily for those serving over you as leaders in the Kingdom?
- ❖ Ask people for their prayers as Paul did (2 Thessalonians 3:1).

Pray

Father God, thank You for my spiritual leaders, teach me to pray for them. Guide my prayers so that these are effective and avail much. Help me to also live under the spiritual covering You have provided for me. In Jesus' name I ask, amen.

Meditate

Remember those who rule over you,
who have spoken the word of God to you,
whose faith follow, considering the outcome of
their conduct.
Hebrews 13:7 NKJV

I urge, then, first of all, that petitions, prayers,
intercession and thanksgiving be made for all
people – for kings and all those in authority,
that we may live peaceful and quiet lives
in all godliness and holiness.
1 Timothy 2:1-3 NIV

Notes

19 Deliberation Necessary to Largest Results from Prayer

Our devotions are not measured by the clock, but time is of their essence. The ability to wait and stay and press belongs essentially to our intercourse with God. Hurry, everywhere unseeming and damaging, is so to an alarming extent in the great business of communion with God. Short devotions are the bane of deep piety. Calmness, grasp, strength, are never the companions of hurry. Short devotions deplete spiritual vigour, arrest spiritual progress, sap spiritual foundations, blight the root and bloom of spiritual life. They are the prolific source of backsliding, the sure indication of a superficial piety; they deceive, blight, rot the seed, and impoverish the soil.

It is true that Bible prayers in word and print are short, but the praying men of the Bible were with God through many a sweet and holy wrestling hour. They won by few words but long waiting. The prayers Moses records may be short, but Moses prayed to God with fastings and mighty cryings forty days and nights.

The statement of Elijah's praying may be condensed to a few brief paragraphs, but doubtless Elijah, who when "praying he prayed," spent many hours of fiery struggle and lofty intercourse with God before he could, with assured boldness, say to Ahab, "There shall not be dew nor rain these years, but according to my word." The verbal brief of Paul's prayers is short, but

Paul "prayed night and day exceedingly." The "Lord's Prayer" is a divine epitome for infant lips, but the man Christ Jesus prayed many and all night ere his work was done; and his all-night and long-sustained devotions gave to his work its finish and perfection, and to his character the fullness and glory of its divinity.

Spiritual work is taxing work, and men are loath to do it. Praying, true praying, costs an outlay of serious attention and of time, which flesh and blood do not relish. Few persons are made of such strong fibre that they will make a costly outlay when surface work will pass as well in the market. We can habituate ourselves to our beggarly praying until it looks well to us, at least it keeps up a decent form and quiets conscience – the deadliest of opiates! We can slight our praying, and not realize the peril till the foundations are gone.

Hurried devotions make weak faith, feeble convictions, questionable piety. To be little with God is to be little for God. To cut short the praying makes the whole religious character short, scrimp, niggardly, and slovenly.

It takes good time for the full flow of God into the spirit. Short devotions cut the pipe of God's full flow. It takes time in the secret places to get the full revelation of God. Little time and hurry mar the picture.

Henry Martyn laments that "want of private devotional reading and shortness of prayer through incessant sermon-making had produced much strangeness between God and his soul." He judged that he had dedicated too much time to public ministrations and too little to private communion with God. He was much impressed to set apart times for fasting and to devote times for solemn prayer. Resulting from this he records: "Was assisted this morning to pray for two hours." Said William Wilberforce, the peer of kings: "I must secure more time for private devotions. I have been living far too public for me. The shortening of private devotions starves the soul; it grows lean and faint. I have been keeping too late hours." Of a failure in Parliament he says: "Let me record my grief and shame, and all, probably, from private devotions having been contracted, and so God let me stumble." More solitude and earlier hours was his remedy.

More time and early hours for prayer would act like magic to revive and invigorate many a decayed spiritual life. More time and early hours for prayer would be manifest in holy living. A holy life would not be so rare or so difficult a thing if our devotions were not so short and hurried. A Christly temper in its sweet and passionless fragrance would not be so alien and hopeless a heritage if our closet stay were lengthened and intensified. We live shabbily because we pray meanly. Plenty of time to feast in our closets will bring marrow and fatness to our lives. Our ability to stay with God in our closet measures our ability to stay with God out of the closet. Hasty closet visits are deceptive, defaulting. We are not only deluded by them, but we are losers by them in many ways and in many rich legacies. Tarrying in the closet instructs and wins. We are taught by it, and the greatest victories are often the results of great waiting – waiting till words and plans are exhausted, and silent and patient waiting gains the crown. Jesus Christ asks with an affronted emphasis, "Shall not God avenge his own elect which cry day and night unto him?"

To pray is the greatest thing we can do: and to do it well there must be calmness, time, and deliberation; otherwise it is degraded into the littlest and meanest of things. True praying has the largest results for good; and poor praying, the least. We cannot do too much of real praying; we cannot do too little of the sham. We must learn anew the worth of prayer, enter anew the school of prayer. There is nothing which it takes more time to learn. And if we would learn the wondrous art, we must not give a fragment here and there – "A little talk with Jesus," as the tiny saintlets sing – but we must demand and hold with iron grasp the best hours of the day for God and prayer, or there will be no praying worth the name.

This, however, is not a day of prayer. Few men there are who pray. Prayer is defamed by preacher and priest. In these days of hurry and bustle, of electricity and steam, men will not take time to pray. Preachers there are who "say prayers" as a part of their programme, on regular or state occasions; but who "stirs himself up to take hold upon God?" Who prays as

Jacob prayed – till he is crowned as a prevailing, princely intercessor? Who prays as Elijah prayed – till all the locked-up forces of nature were unsealed and a famine-stricken land bloomed as the garden of God? Who prayed as Jesus Christ prayed as out upon the mountain he "continued all night in prayer to God?" The apostles "gave themselves to prayer" – the most difficult thing to get men or even the preachers to do. Laymen there are who will give their money – some of them in rich abundance – but they will not "give themselves" to prayer, without which their money is but a curse. There are plenty of preachers who will preach and deliver great and eloquent addresses on the need of revival and the spread of the kingdom of God, but not many there are who will do that without which all preaching and organizing are worse than vain – pray. It is out of date, almost a lost art, and the greatest benefactor this age could have is the man who will bring the preachers and the Church back to prayer.

Reflect

How can you be intentional and thoughtful in your prayers, aiming for specific and significant outcomes?

- Using the apostolic prayers found in the Bible could be a great tool.
- Using lists to refer to when praying (perhaps having a different list for each day of the week).
- Using the Lord's Prayer in Matthew 6 as a template for prayer.

Pray

Father God, teach me how to wait upon You. Teach me to persevere in intercession like Jacob did, until I have Your assurance of having received or until I see the answer to the prayers You put on my heart. In Jesus' name I ask, amen.

Meditate

...You do not have because you do not ask God. When you ask, you do not receive, because you ask with wrong motives, that you may spend what you get on your pleasures.

James 4:2b-3 NIV

Therefore, I urge you, brothers and sisters, in view of God's mercy, to offer your bodies as a living sacrifice, holy and pleasing to God – this is your true and proper worship.

Romans 12:1 NIV

Notes

20 A Praying Pulpit Begets a Praying Pew

Only glimpses of the great importance of prayer could the apostles get before Pentecost. But the Spirit coming and filling on Pentecost elevated prayer to its vital and all-commanding position in the gospel of Christ. The call now of prayer to every saint is the Spirit's loudest and most exigent call. Sainthood's piety is made, refined, perfected, by prayer. The gospel moves with slow and timid pace when the saints are not at their prayers early and late and long.

Where are the Christly leaders who can teach the modern saints how to pray and put them at it? Do we know we are raising up a prayerless set of saints? Where are the apostolic leaders who can put God's people to praying? Let them come to the front and do the work, and it will be the greatest work which can be done. An increase of educational facilities and a great increase of money force will be the direst curse to religion if they are not sanctified by more and better praying than we are doing. More praying will not come as a matter of course. The campaign for the twentieth or thirtieth century fund will not help our praying but hinder if we are not careful. Nothing but a specific effort from a praying leadership will avail. The chief ones must lead in the apostolic effort to radicate the vital importance and fact of prayer in the heart and life of the Church. None but praying leaders can have praying followers. Praying apostles will beget praying saints. A praying pulpit will beget praying pews. We do greatly need somebody who can set the saints to this business of praying. We are not a generation of praying saints. Non-praying saints are a beggarly gang of saints who have neither the ardour nor the beauty nor the power of saints. Who will restore this breach? The greatest will he be of reformers and apostles, who can set the Church to praying.

We put it as our most sober judgment that the great need of the Church in this and all ages is men of such commanding faith, of such unsullied holiness, of such marked spiritual vigour and consuming zeal, that their prayers, faith, lives, and ministry will be of such a radical and aggressive form as to work spiritual revolutions which will form eras in individual and Church life.

We do not mean men who get up sensational stirs by novel devices, nor those who attract by a pleasing entertainment; but men who can stir things, and work revolutions by the preaching of God's Word and by the power of the Holy Ghost, revolutions which change the whole current of things.

Natural ability and educational advantages do not figure as factors in this matter; but capacity for faith, the ability to pray, the power of thorough consecration, the ability of self-littleness, an absolute losing of one's self in God's glory, and an ever-present and insatiable yearning and seeking after all the fullness of God – men who can set the Church ablaze for God; not in a noisy, showy way, but with an intense and quiet heat that melts and moves everything for God.

God can work wonders if he can get a suitable man. Men can work wonders if they can get God to lead them. The full endowment of the spirit that turned the world upside down would be eminently useful in these latter days. Men who can stir things mightily for God, whose spiritual revolutions change the whole aspect of things, are the universal need of the Church.

The Church has never been without these men; they adorn its history; they are the standing miracles of the divinity of the Church; their example and history are an unfailing inspiration and blessing. An increase in their number and power should be our prayer.

That which has been done in spiritual matters can be done again, and be better done. This was Christ's view. He said "Verily, verily, I say unto you, He that believeth on me, the works that I do shall he do also; and greater works than these shall he do; because I go unto my Father." The past has not exhausted the possibilities nor the demands for doing great things for God. The Church that is dependent on its past history for its miracles of power and grace is a fallen Church.

God wants elect men – men out of whom self and the world have gone by a severe crucifixion, by a bankruptcy which has so totally ruined self and the world that there is neither hope nor desire of recovery; men who by this insolvency and crucifixion have turned toward God perfect hearts.

Let us pray ardently that God's promise to prayer may be more than realized.

Reflect

Can you think of two ways to cultivate a culture of prayer within your church, starting from the leadership down to every member?

- If there is no regular prayer meeting, beginning one is a good place to start.
- Build meaningful prayer into the public services.
- Encourage members to read books on prayer.
- Teach a sermon series on prayer.

Pray

Father God, here are my heart, my lips and my body to do Your work in my generation. Set in my heart a zeal for Your Body, and guide me into how I may help build up a praying culture in my local church. In Jesus' name I ask, amen.

Meditate

"But when you pray, go into your room, close the door and pray to your Father, who is unseen. Then your Father, who sees what is done in secret, will reward you."

Matthew 6:6 NIV

"Again I say to you that if two of you agree on earth concerning anything that they ask, it will be done for them by My Father in heaven. For where two or three are gathered together in My name, I am there in the midst of them."

Matthew 18:19-20 NKJV

"these I will bring to my holy mountain and give them joy in my house of prayer. Their burnt offerings and sacrifices will be accepted on my altar; for my house will be called a house of prayer for all nations."

Isaiah 56:7 NIV

Notes

Notes

Notes

Notes

Notes

Notes

Notes

Notes

Notes

Notes

Notes

Notes